Advance Praise fo

M000103838

You have touched on some critical areas that everyone needs to take seriously: finding a job that's not a job but an opportunity that fulfills oneself; keeping skills sharp and learning new skills to keep up with our fast-moving society; and realizing it's not all about the money but how change can have a positive impact on life and career.

I can see this book benefiting not only mature workers/baby boomers but future generations of workers who will be entering a totally different workforce than those who went before them. This book, because of its positive message and encouragement, cannot help but be a success. It provides an opportunity to individuals to recognize what responsibility for self is all about, as well as offering positive techniques to change negative mind-sets and attitudes. It provides a road map to self-discovery and the art of making good, well-thought-out choices. In addition it provides the reader with the knowledge that they are not out there alone, they are of value, and there are opportunities in abundance if they are willing to change and move forward.

Rosemary Smith, PHR, CWDP, Pima County One Stop Career Center

Put Your Spirit to Work by Deborah Knox is a blending of the past, the present, and the future. It looks at the past and how various management styles play a part in determining your present and future career path decisions. Ms. Knox then goes into how to determine where you are now and why that is important to understanding your core competencies. Finally, by looking at the future you can see where to go to find the dream job you have been searching for. I highly recommend this for any individual struggling to find their way in today's difficult social and economic environment.

Lola Kakes, CEO and founder of EffortlessHR,
author of *If You Don't Own a Circus ... You Shouldn't Be Hiring Clowns!*

For many of us baby boomers who started our careers in a paradigm created by our father's generation, it can be mind-boggling to understand today's work environment. In *Put Your Spirit to Work*, Deborah helps us to not just see how things have changed, but to understand why the changes are beneficial to us, the workers. Now is the time to embrace the changes and take advantage of the opportunities they offer to our lives.

Beth Schecher, Schecher Management Consulting

An absolute must-read book for anyone who is experiencing a life transition. Deborah Knox provides solid advice, tips, and resources for restructuring your career and life. She has written a down-to-earth, inspiring, and amazingly useful guide for anyone who needs inspiration and practical wisdom from an expert. I enjoyed reading it very much, and took a lot of the advice to heart for my own life and career.

Mikaela Quinn, founding publisher and editor
of the *Tucson Green Times* and the *New Southwest* newspaper

Put Your Spirit to Work

Put Your Spirit to Work

Making a Living Being Yourself

DEBORAH KNOX

Put Your Spirit to Work: Making a Living Being Yourself

Published by Wheatmark®
1760 East River Road, Suite 145
Tucson, Arizona 85718 USA
www.wheatmark.com

ISBN: 978-1-60494-660-4
LCCN: 2011938527

rev201201

Contents

STEP #1

Telling Your Story

45

STEP #2

Defining Core Competencies

59

STEP #3

Redefining Your Self
85

STEP #4

Goal Setting
105

STEP #5

Pulling Together Your Profile

113

Acknowledgements

Why do we do what we do? It's a question that has fascinated me for most of my adult life. And what does that have to do with how we each earn a living? Is your work fulfilling and as rewarding as it can be? If you're one of those seeking to find your life work purpose, this book gives me the opportunity to share with you the motivating tools, checklists, exercises, and updated information on the newly emerging workforce.

I'm one of the fortunate ones who discovered my life work early on and continue to make a living doing work that I love. For over thirty years I have been blessed with meaningful work.

The path to meaningful work comes in answering the following question: "What needs doing in your world?" Finding *your* answer to that question (and many more included here) provides a clue to what is rewarding and fulfilling to you. More than ever before, we need to find new ways of working that are true, consistent, and authentically represent our individual skills, interests, values, purpose, and personal rewards. The world of work has shifted so much, and the old traditional means of finding employment are no longer obvious. But what needs doing is obvious everywhere we look. This book is dedicated to the thousands of people out there who want to make a difference doing work you love.

Thanks to those who have supported the continuation of my life work:

Sandra Butzel, coauthor of the first edition of *Life Work Transitions.com: Putting Your Spirit Online*, who encouraged me to bring the second edition to the marketplace. Kay Sather provided the brilliant cover design that captures the past and the present so well. Gail McMeekin, Lin Ormondroyd, Nancy Brook, and Beth Schecher make sure I keep putting my spirit to work. And I'm grateful to my family and friends in New England and the Southwest who share the joy and challenge of doing work we love.

Introduction

So, you brave souls who have picked up this book, what does it mean to you to "put your spirit to work?" And what do we mean by *spirit*?

In answering the call to put your spirit to work, I refer to *spirit* as the ancient Hebrew term *ruah*, which means "breath," and therefore spirit is the essence of who we are, uniquely and individually. It's that simple. *The Oxford English Dictionary* has this definition for spirit: "The animating or vital principle in humans and animals; that which gives life to the physical organism, in contrast to its purely material elements; the breath of life."

Life work is the manifestation of the essential self in that area of your life considered work, as in being paid to do what you love to do. Work also provides the means to meet the most basic of human needs: food, safety, and security. Unfortunately, due to the financial disaster of 2008, an increasing number of hard-working souls are just barely meeting their survival needs or are seriously worried about the future due to a reduction in income at that time. Who would have thought we would be here now? Who ever thought this would happen to the generation that ended a war?

And so you find yourself asking the question "Where do I go from here with my life?" Whether you are asking the question at twenty-two or sixty-two years of age, you will discover more about what it means to you to put your spirit to work within the pages of this book.

Chapter One: Putting Your Spirit to Work in the Twenty-First Century is a revised and updated edition of *Life Work Transitions.com: Putting Your Spirit Online*. It provides some tools for mastering the new world of work. For those of you who understand the value and importance of engaging in meaningful work, the information based on Abraham Maslow's work will provide a solid model for self-actualizing in the workplace. William Bridges, author of *Transitions: Making Sense of Life's Changes*, offers a model for dealing with change that will be helpful in navigating the new employment reality. The Career Management Competencies have been updated to include the necessary skills for being successfully self-employed; according to the Entrepreneurs' Source at http://www.entrepreneurssource.com/blog.html, the self-employed now constitute at least 35 percent of the employed workforce. I've also included Daniel Pink's "six senses required to meet the new employment challenges" as cited in his recent book *A Whole New Mind:* http://danpink.com.

The new mind-set requires realizing and accepting the ongoing changes in the world of work and new ways of looking at the market and employability. Because the markets have shifted, many of the jobs in the old economy are never going to come back. People are advised to lower their expectations when jobs are scarce and take whatever they can get. But what's really required is to flip that paradigm and become part of the solution to the problem of "where are the jobs" and to start creating your own. If you knew: a) what mattered to you, b) what you cared about, and c) how you would uniquely address it you would be in a much better position to focus your energy and attention. Now is the time to do that.

You will confront both fear and opportunities as you navigate the current landscape called the world of work. The information included on the *Nine Stages of Career Development* will help you to understand your development needs, which will guide you in making the choices about when to compromise and when to continue your search for something better. For those seeking a somewhat more spiritual approach, a review of the energy chakra systems may provide additional grounding for what's frequently known as the roller-coaster ride. These are not easy choices, but you will be better prepared to make them after you have identified what your meaningful life work will be.

Chapter Two: Finding Your True North provides you with the tools and questions to discover your meaningful life work. Through a systematic process, you will be able to find the answers that will guide you to put your spirit to work. It's a process that takes some time (four to six weeks), focusing four to ten hours a week, approximately. You can breeze through it faster, but why bother? Take the time to get it right this time. Take the time to be honest with yourself. If not now, when?

The baby boomer cohort, from ages forty-seven to sixty-six, are making significantly different career choices based on whether they are in the forty-seven to fifty-six age group or the fifty-seven to sixty-six age group. Both have suffered significantly as a result of the recent economic downturn, which affected people's retirement plans and now is forcing them to create new career plans. What both groups have in common, however, is the need to create and respond to new trends influencing finding and creating meaningful work. The ways people find jobs and the kind of jobs that are available, as well as the physical workplace, are in the midst of constant change. Developing the tools to stay on the edge of any trend will help you to not only survive, but to thrive in the new world of work. We focus on that by guiding you to expand and clarify the self-definition of who you are and what you bring to the world of work.

The search for meaning and finding it can finally be the goal for all of us who want to continue working and making a difference. For those who have all the stuff they need, meaning is the new money. For over five hundred million *"cultural creatives,"* who insist on "seeing the big picture, value empathy, see personal experience as valuable, and demonstrate an ethic of caring for others and the environment" (Paul Ray, *Cultural Creatives: How 50 Million People are Changing the World*, 2001), the search for meaning in work is a key ingredient that must be met. (And in case you haven't noticed, *meaning* is translated to *mission* in today's most successful companies attracting and retaining the best and the brightest.)

For this generation and those that follow, it is time to declare our legacy and start communicating with those in their twenties and thirties who experience a similar longing for meaningful and transformative work. The focus on meaning and purpose is necessary to succeed in today's expanded global market. For every individual there is a world of work that only needs to be discovered. The new global market, with its environmental, humanitarian, and economic challenges, is in need of all of our gifts, talents, expected rewards, and unique perspective. The culmination of this section is the creation of a personal mandala—the beginning and evolving definition of putting your spirit to work.

Finally, having identified your life work objective, you are ready to explore the external world that calls you. In **Chapter Three: Putting Your Spirit to Work: Exploring the World of Work** we teach you the skills for effectively conducting career and market research. Most likely you've already started to do some research, but now you'll want to direct your exploration into the external and virtual world of work in a more systematic way. We provide our proven steps for researching career options to identify careers/industries, individuals, and organizations for you to contact. As you deepen your knowledge of the field, the people, and the most relevant issues that match your concerns and talents, you will better be able to define and brand yourself using the latest social media tools.

Using the tools of networking and informational interviewing, you will approach individuals to find out more about your field of interest and hopefully obtain referrals to decision makers. Building a network online and in person requires adapting to the latest technology and including social media in your campaign. This high-tech option offers some exciting tools for connecting with individuals and conducting research online, and is essential for conducting a thorough job search. We present the guidelines for conducting networking and informational interviews in a way that will make you feel and be successful. Learning the technology and being able to present yourself authentically using this medium will expand your network greatly and provide additional information from the traditional research methods outlined in this chapter.

In the past ten years, the trends and opportunities for employment have changed, and the business of dealing with change has become more important than ever. Life work transitions occur frequently, and there is a need to stay centered in your life as you successfully navigate these changes. Finding and putting your spirit to work will provide you with the means to master these changes. *Thanks* for picking up this book. I don't think you'll be sorry you did.

Websites Referenced

The Entrepreneur's Source
www.entrepreneurssource.com

Dan Pink
www.danpink.com

1

Putting Your Spirit to Work in the Twenty-First Century

Are you yearning to know and express your unique talents in response to some critical need in society? Do you feel you have something special at your core that can guide and lead you on the path of right livelihood, if you only knew how to begin that journey? Would you like to be proactive and self-directed in managing life work transitions? From time immemorial, mystics and theologians have studied the universal search for purpose and belonging that calls us. Today, this quest takes place in the work world and in the spaces that exist between employment opportunities—life work transitions.

In addition to internal drive, the new work ethic of the twenty-first century and the new workplace will be defined and driven by those individuals who possess personal vision, a strong sense of professional responsibility, and the technical expertise to access a global marketplace. This book provides a unique opportunity and guide for a spiritual and practical exploration of your life and career, resulting in a clearly stated yet comprehensive career and life work objective that is flexible, lasting, and deeply personal. You will also learn how to manage the information that leads to knowledge and wisdom by assessing, selecting, and prioritizing important criteria. One of the greatest challenges facing us is to create work that will provide meaning as well as the means of earning a livelihood. Many individuals have been downsized from corporate America in the prime of their careers. Others are being forced to retire early and, on losing the long-sought pension plan, must find alternative means of employment. This may come in the form of a similar job in a related field. However, some will feel called to address the deeper issues of finding meaningful work that mirrors the inner desire and the outer realities facing us as the new millennium unfolds.

The Individual in Transition

If you are convinced that there is more to work than earning a living, this book is for you. If you feel a certain power guiding you, and you yearn to connect with it, this book is for you. If you believe in karma or destiny and want to look for the miracles in the every-dayness of your work world, this book is for you. If you believe there is a unique spark of the divine in each of us, and you want to participate in workplaces that hold and practice that belief, this book is for you. If you feel driven to speak your truth about some deeply held personal belief and find it suddenly attached to a cause far greater than yourself, this book will help you focus your energies. If you believe there are no longer jobs to compete for, this book will help you create meaningful alternatives.

After working in one field, perhaps you find expectations and rewards have shifted dramatically. Perhaps money is no longer the sole motivator, and customer feedback is less fulfilling. You may lack a vision about the relevance and purpose of what you do, or perhaps your heart grows dim when you perceive a situation of waste, neglect, or abuse. You desperately want to make a difference but lack the confidence or knowledge to proceed. You can find meaning and purpose by defining and creating a personal vision statement that will give you a focus and direction. The need to know what we are called to do can catapult us onto the path of discovery.

If you are between employment opportunities, by choice or necessity, it is important to understand where you are in your transition cycle in order to maximize the energy you have available. Likewise, if you are dealing with a major life transition, such as losing a job, having to move, or experiencing a major illness, you will be able to better handle the transition by becoming aware of the feeling stages

Think of this exploration process as both internal and external. Internally you are seeking the core truth that will allow you to find and express your true voice. Externally in our society, the disappearance of traditional jobs and career ladders, the restructuring of the workplace, and the increased use of technology will provide new opportunities for finding and creating meaningful work. In order to survive, we must have work, yet in order to thrive, we must have meaningful work.

Is This the Path for You?

Do you have a need to express your unique purpose and wisdom? Is there a longing to find your true expression and have work you love? The truth will reveal itself as a result of your persistence in following the journey outlined in chapter two. It all begins with intention—if you are seeking to find true meaning, purpose, and passion in your life work, then you will find it. Therefore you decide to take this journey now, because if you don't you will never know, and the world may not gain what you have to offer. The power of that concept is reflected in the words of Martha Graham, the influential American dancer, teacher, and choreographer of modern dance, whose ballets and other words were intended to reveal the inner man:

> There is a vitality, a life-force, an energy, a quickening, which is translated through you into action. And because there is only one of you in all time, this expression is unique, and if you block it, it will never exist through any other medium, ... and the world will not have it.

One of the most profound results of undertaking this journey is becoming aware of the serendipitous events in your life as you learn to recognize and trust the natural unfolding of your life's pattern. In *The Soul's Code*, James Hillman, a Jungian analyst, refers to the acorn image to illustrate that the entire potential of our life's destiny is in a tiny seed. How we grow the tree and utilize and develop that potential is one of our most basic and blessed responsibilities. Undertaking this journey of career exploration, while learning our life lessons, will help develop the insight and personal responsibility required in the new world of work. If you hope to have this kind of knowing and find your right livelihood, you may have realized there are many false prophets and paths beckoning to you. As Frederick Buechner wrote in *Wishful Thinking: A Seeker's ABC*:

> There are all different kinds of voices calling you to do all different kinds of work, and the problem is to find out which is the voice of God, rather than that of society, say, or the superego, or self-interest. By and large, a good rule for finding this out is the following: the kind of work God usually calls you to is the kind of work: a/that you need most to do, and b/ that the world needs most to have done. If you really get a kick out of your work, you've presumably met requirement a/, but if your work is writing deodorant commercials, the chances are you've missed requirement b/. On the other hand, if your work is being a doctor in a leper colony, you've probably met requirement b/, but if most of the time you're bored and depressed by your work, the chances are that you've not only bypassed a/, but probably aren't helping your patients much either.... The place God calls you to is the place where your deep gladness and the world's deep hunger meet.

Finding work you love is the discovery of your deep gladness. By thoughtfully clarifying your skills, goals, values, rewards, and interests through this journey of self-discovery, you will discern your deep gladness, the full expression of yourself. By defining your passions and your concerns, you will identify areas where the world is hungry for service or attention. The place God calls you to in the world, where you can exchange skills and energy, is your marketplace.

The Twenty-First-Century Workplace

In the early 1970s, John Crystal coauthored *Where Do I Go from Here with My Life?* with Richard Bolles, and they introduced the concept that work was originally created to meet unmet societal needs. He was talking about creating work, not necessarily finding jobs. In 1989, in his groundbreaking book *The Age of Unreason*, Charles Handy introduced the concept of portfolio work to replace the concept of linear career progression. The illustrative example he used to demonstrate this concept was of the actor/director in theater who would take on any role that came along in order to survive and thrive in the field, all the while accumulating skills and experience for the one blockbuster event. This innovative concept is employed regularly by entrepreneurs, consultants, and craftspeople who have developed successful business strategies that consist of using multiple portfolios of skill sets to address different customer needs and alternative reward systems, all while pursuing a larger vision. The current downsizing of corporate America establishes the portfolio career as an emerging trend for the future. No longer will we be employed by one company, let alone remain in one career or one job. (See http://www.globalideasbank.org for some new, fresh ideas.)

We need to see ourselves as self-employed and responsible for developing our own portfolios. As Handy says, "Portfolios accumulate by chance. They should accumulate by choice. We can manage our time. We can say no. We can give less priority, or more, to homework or paid work. Money is essential, but more money is not always essential. Enough can be enough. Without deliberate choice, portfolios can become too full." The process of career and life work planning involves you making deliberate choices. This practice sets the stage for discernment leading to right action and right livelihood.

The New Employment Reality

Before you begin the journey of self-discovery, and of your rightful place in the universe, let us look at the current state of work in the twenty-first century. There is a new employment contract that stresses flexible employment opportunities and preparedness rather than job security. This new focus on individuals taking personal responsibility for managing their work lives will actually create more employment opportunities. The resulting flexibility and mobility comes from being able to rearrange multiple skill sets to fit changing work structures and target a vast array of markets to utilize your skills and knowledge base. The new employment contract requires you to develop and maintain the following practices in order to acquire mastery. You will have the rest of your life to fine-tune them!

1. Know yourself as "Me, Inc.," possessing a portfolio of multiple skill sets that can be applied in a variety of settings.

2. Know the appropriate skill sets and functions in your fields of interest. Look for what needs doing. Forget job titles. Seek projects.

3. Know your field. Stay current through professional associations, networking, and knowledge management.

4. Know your current skill sets (and your desired future) and identify a training process for developing competencies and knowledge that will increase your "value added" and your overall marketability.

5. Know your customers and the changing demands of the marketplace. Demonstrate curiosity and initiative to learn about their real needs and changing values.

6. Know your department or specialty and the changing demands of the marketplace, internal and external customers, vendors, and the politics of your industry.

7. Know your competition and collaborators. Develop relations that foster mutual learning and respect and encourage the brokering of services rendered. Think of yourself as a cocreator of valued goods and services.

8. Know how to lead change. Develop a proactive attitude. Take responsibility for managing personal transitions and anticipating change.

The new employment reality requires you to learn to manage your career. Cliff Hakim, in his book *We Are All Self-Employed*, first introduced the concept of the "career lattice" as opposed to the career ladder that formerly defined traditional career growth and development. The latter was based on a natural progression of jobs largely defined by the hierarchical workplace of the 1960s and 1970s. Good performance often resulted in promotions, increased wages, and opportunities to grow within the organization. The organization was responsible for fulfilling this structure. Hakim's lattice approach (similar to Handy's portfolio) applies to the new organizations that structure themselves with less hierarchy and more of a team environment, where lateral moves are encouraged to develop skill sets. For those individuals who remain outside the formal employment system, the portfolio skill development approach places the responsibility for ongoing career development in the hearts and minds of the individual seeking new projects.

The 1980s brought full employment, cross-functional teams, and multidisciplinary training, urging the hierarchy to disassemble itself. The incredible flush and productivity of that era was replaced quite dramatically by the downsizing of the 1990s, which has left literally thousands out of the traditional workplace. Middle-management jobs were some of the first to go in those industries that had been the mainstay of our economy. They were replaced by a generation of computers giving managers direct access to all information without reports being funneled through middle management. Individuals must now find opportunities within their organization or department where they can make a real contribution. Lateral moves rather than promotions become attractive because they offer new opportunities to learn important skills and expand the possibilities for employment. The new employment reality teaches us to focus on projects and tasks at hand. This may mean seeking out new projects, relationships, and knowledge in order to expand opportunities. The notion of continuous learning is key for the worker of tomorrow. In order to continue to learn and thrive, individuals must conduct self-assessment exercises and update their portfolios regularly in order to move forward.

And most recently, the Great Recession of 2008 has impacted even further the changing dynamics of where the jobs are. In this huge global transition, the total economic system and job creation functions will be changing. Individuals must navigate a system that is unstable as they look for sustainable opportunities. For the mature worker, this period of time provides the opportunity to creatively pursue new paths for meeting financial and life purpose goals, while building on the vast experience that's been acquired. In partnership with the younger generation, new business opportunities are being created, and once again we realize you're part of the problem if you're not part of the solution. So, for those who have lost more than their share of pension funds (or never had any because you were too busy doing the work you love), the necessity of reinventing yourself has never been greater. And while you're at it, you can help to reinvent the new economy as well as the new workplace.

Career Management and Self Employment Competencies

Knowing yourself as possessing a portfolio of multiple skill sets will allow you to take advantage of multiple career opportunities. Learning and developing the career management and self-employment competencies to implement the new employment contract will ensure you lifelong learning and earning possibilities. Learning and developing these competencies is the cornerstone of successful career mastery. Increasingly, the successfully employed individual needs to not only possess mastery in a technical/functional or knowledge area, but must also possess the skills for communicating, marketing, and demonstrating that expertise.

Career Assessment—Today's knowledgeable worker realizes that career management is an ongoing part of one's professional development.

Self-Management—The personal is professional, and the more authentic you can be in terms of work style and personal values, the better for you. Bringing your spirit to work in the twenty-first century requires the ability to demonstrate initiative and work independently with increasing awareness of the larger community.

Interpersonal and Facilitation—These skills demonstrate insight into motivating human behavior and focusing on relationship building in acquiring new work. They are also important in communicating with partners, vendors, and customers across the board.

Project Management—For the unemployed or the employed, project management skills allow you to work with others to get the job done and to partner with others in accomplishing results. Manage and acquire information and resources, trouble-shoot, and plan.

Planning and Decision Making—When we are clear on our priorities, we make better decisions, but we also need a clear plan or vision and criteria. The ability to establish a structure that encourages individual responsibility is an essential tool.

Leadership—As a leader to collaborators, customers, and other consultants in your field or business community, you excel at creating long-lasting relationships and are a recognized leader in your field. You are able to empower others and are willing to cocreate and share the results.

Computer Technology—The ability to learn new databases and technology, conduct online research, and integrate the latest social media is a key determinant of successful employability.

Growth and Development—There is a need for a plan for continuous self-development and lifelong learning. We need to stay passionate about our subject matter and motivated from within to master these skills as well as others essential to performance.

Creativity and Visioning—You'll need this skill set to initiate new activities and to create a buzz of originality to your products and services. The ability to act on something so compelling that it's right in front of you, the intuitive knowing what can and must be done, and the ability to initiate, develop, and maintain ideas and synthesize, adapt, and improve.

Time Management—Time is the most personal tool for transformation. The continuum of activities that you are responsible for on a daily basis requires the ability to manage your time, this most precious resource. Use it wisely.

Portfolio careers and the demands of Workforce 2000 speak to the need for individuals to think of themselves as being self-employed. By not relying on one single employer, let alone the naive belief that one career will last a lifetime, we are required to become more independent and resourceful. By developing and practicing the competencies outlined above, the individual will be able to successfully navigate the uncharted waters of the twenty-first century.

Redefining Work

There is plenty of work to be done even if the jobs are disappearing and the traditional workplace is changing. There will be more giant organizations resulting from ongoing mergers and many new entrepreneurial ventures resulting from individual vision and initiative. Matthew Fox, in his *Re-invention of Work*, encourages us to think about redefining work to be more inclusive, humane, and dignified. This twentieth-century radical priest says that "to live well is to work well." Having meaningful work is about meeting unmet societal needs, engaging in self-expression, and creating mutual exchanges of energy and value. Work should allow us to make a difference in the moments of our daily life, as well as on a global level. Work needs to be about creating and caring for community. Creating your life work requires your unique expression. Individually each of us needs to exercise personal responsibility if we are to ensure our collective survival.

Because the workplace is temporal and defined by current reality, we cannot ignore the forces or the effects of the current downsizing and elimination of jobs. Indeed, if you are reading this, you may well be one of the ones who is existing in the space between work. You are in the middle of a major life transition. Somehow you are managing, but you feel a strong lack of purpose and meaning. At the same time, you see an emergence of many new fields, companies, and opportunities. By exploring what needs doing in your world and being attuned to the ever-changing marketplace of the twenty-first century, you will be engaged in the all important process of redefining, reinventing, and revaluing work and self. As individuals assume responsibility for this, we will find ourselves realigning our societal values and definition of work. No government agency can do this for us, and the employers need workers to lead the way.

As we learned during the 1960s, and still find true today, the personal is political. Being personal at work means discovering our "deep gladness." When we experience congruency between values, beliefs, and behaviors, we produce enhanced results. By defining your criteria that ensure the full expression of who you are, you will be redefining and reinventing work—for yourself first and then for others, by example.

The impetus for change grows daily, according to Jeremy Rifkin in *The End of Work*. Because of restructuring and merger-mania, many jobs have completely disappeared, and he sees no real growth areas for wage work. The prescription for change lies within each of us, even in the low-paying service sector, where individuals who consciously follow this process to identify meaningful personal criteria will fare better than those who are unaware of the power of personal choice.

The final tool for dealing with the new workplace is from Daniel Pink's recent book, *A Whole New Mind*, where he asks the question: Why will right-brainers rule the future? He suggests that in order to survive in this new age, individuals and organizations must examine what they're doing to earn a living and ask themselves three questions:

1. Can someone overseas do it cheaper?

2. Can a computer do it faster?

3. Is what I'm offering in demand in an age of abundance?

The drivers of the change requiring the new worker mentality are Abundance, Asia, and Automation as well as changes driven by the demographics of the Cultural Creatives who are looking for a new kind of meaning from their work. The paradigm for the new workplace is High Concept = High Touch, which results in a more right-brain/creative approach to the way we work and think.

To meet the challenges of the new era he says the following six senses are needed:

1. Not just function, but DESIGN—things need to be beautiful, whimsical, and emotionally engaging.

2. Not just argument, but also STORY—information overload with facts is not enough; we need the essence of persuasion, communication, and self-understanding to tell a compelling narrative.

3. Not just focus, but also SMYPHONY—beyond specialization and now needing to pull the pieces together—not analysis, but synthesis—seeing the big picture, crossing boundaries, and being able to combine disparate pieces into an arresting new whole.

4. Not just logic, but also EMPATHY—what makes others tick, the ability to forge relationships and to care for others.

5. Not just seriousness, but also PLAY—Health and professional benefits of laughter, lightheartedness, games, and humor; we all need to play.

6. Not just accumulation, but also MEANING—too much materialism, and now we need to pursue more significant desires, such as purpose, transcendence, and spiritual fulfillment.

These six senses share a lot of characteristics with the previous listing of competencies and will help you create a portfolio of skills to survive and thrive in today's workplace. I'm grateful to Dan for allowing me to share this information and encourage you to take a look at his book for specific means for developing these senses to increase your career management ability (http://www.danpink. com).

Another excellent reference he cites for more specific information on the new labor force is the work of Frank Levy, *The New Division of Labor: How Computers Are Creating the Next Job Market*. He notes that the greatest area of job growth is in jobs requiring interpersonal skills and emotional intelligence, such as nursing, while imagination and creativity are employed by graphic designers. In addition, the following two skill sets are also indicated as essential for survival in the twenty-first century: "expert thinking—solving new problems for which there are no routine solutions"; the other is "complex communication—persuading, explaining, and conveying a particular interpretation of information."

Other Models of Influence

The career life work planning process for mastering change that is presented in chapter two is closely aligned with several other human growth and development models. These theoretical models may serve as guideposts on your journey, offering assurance and reference points if you feel lost. In addition to the first model of transition presented earlier, this next model looks at the typical stages of career development. You can use this model to assess where you are in relation to developing authority and autonomy through your life work. The other models that follow will help you as you journey to develop more of your potential in the spiritual and personal areas of your life.

Nine Stages of Career Development

The nine stage model was originally researched and defined by William Perry and Lee Knefelkamp in the 1970s. I am grateful to Robert J. Ginn Jr. for allowing me to share his insights from "Discovering Your Career Life-Cycle," a manuscript and keynote address presented at the Radcliffe Career Services 80th Anniversary. According to Bob, "the model speaks clearly to the fear and hysteria which is becoming more and more the daily bread of workers in these last years of the 20th century." You may find yourself resonating with more than one of these stages based on your current circumstances, your chronological age, and the amount and variety of work experience to date.

We discover from the introduction by Robert J. Ginn Jr. that: "Unless we understand the forces that shape the way we think and act in our vocations, it is difficult to gain control over our career path. When we learn to direct our life energy toward achieving personal growth and vocational authenticity, we resist the loss of identity associated with joblessness and we stop wasting the abilities with which we are gifted. We also retain the wonderful joy we churn out of the process of growing in vocational self-understanding."

Developing an awareness of the nine stages will help you develop spiritually and personally as well as vocationally. The reference points depicting the various stages include some behaviors that may indicate stuck or rigid styles of thinking, as well as awareness of new behaviors and insights that will create growth and development. See if you can find the truths that you have experienced in the past, and where you might be now as a prelude to creating your life work.

Stage One: Absolute Reliance on External Authority

- Two main assumptions: there is a right career and there is an authority that knows what the right career is; therefore, one will not leave a career unless what they are leaving is bad and there is hope of something better.

- Fewer employers are willing to provide the kind of security that people at this stage feel is necessary. They want adaptive specialists who can manage their own career and move quickly from one area to another as companies respond to rapid changes in the economy.

Stage Two: Awareness of the Possibility of a "Wrong" Decision

- Still feels an external authority in life will define the correct career choice.

- Begins to trust in a process of understanding one's past, abilities, and motivators. A willingness to explore and clarify the impact of genetic programming, social situation, and a complex self. Knowing these biases is the prerequisite to personal freedom.

- Realizes whatever shatters their worldview is telling them that wrong choices are possible and no one's fault.

- Often arises from the broken pieces of a shattered worldview;

for example, jobless PhDs or the disillusionment of layoffs through downsizing.

Stage Three: Substitution of the Process as Authority

- Deals with disillusionment from discovery that career development is not as simple as previously thought.

- Shift from belief that one authority exists to belief that the right decision-making process will yield the right career. The process becomes the authority.

- Continued allegiance to the concept that one right career exists leads to following the "right" process to avoid making mistakes.

Stage Four: Awareness of Multiple "Good" Decisions

- Abandonment of the constructs of one authority and right career.

- Discovery that one can be involved in the process of one's career development.

- Big cognitive flip: the individual rather than the authority authors lists of priorities. She is able to look back on her life story and see the ways vocational self-concept is flowing, growing, and changing.

- May begin feeling the oppression of freedom, too many options.

Stage Five: Emergence of Self as Decision Maker

- Develops internal sense of self as the decision maker and responsible for the choices of life.

- Experiences the reality that vocational identity is determined internally by a moral consciousness based on decision and values clarification and to a much lesser extent by socially defined roles.

- Acceptance of being in charge; this exhilarating, exploring, and doing phase recognizes multiple possibilities and the need to create personal order and clarification.

- Accepts the need to be clear about what needs to be done and the need for feedback about how well one is doing.

Stage Six: Awareness of the Chaos of Free Choice

- "Pride goeth before a fall." Learns about luck, accident, and illness. Temptation to trade authenticity and integrity for security.

- All the alternatives feel like a burden and that life is in chaos.

- Discrepancy between what is desired and what is actually happening creates an inner tension; resolution of tension is the basic barometer of maturity and mental health.

- Challenges and crises promote growth but are often painful.

Stage Seven: Beginnings of Integration of Self and Career Role

- Second cognitive flip: end of polarized career identity. Choosing a traditionally defined role is abandoned in favor of seeing career as a form of self-expression.

- Look at careers as events with certain regularities and with enormous variations and freedom. Responsible for vocational actions, living in light of potential.

- Career is an expression of identity rather than the reverse, where identity is derived from career role or institutional affiliation. Discover the core of vocational freedom. "We are more than what we do."

- Requires some clarity about what one stands for. Realization that life is constructed by us out of our own existential commitments to values, to people, to the kind of self we would be, to our part in the unfolding complexity of life, and to the acquisition and exercise of certain skills consistent with all of the above.

Stage Eight: Experiencing Commitment

- Taking responsibility for the creation of career means also taking responsibility for the undesired outcomes.

- Begins to see that powerlessness, loneliness, fear, pain, and rejection are part of life. Following your bliss is not always blissful, and doubts can come in.

- Learns that life becomes serene and enjoyable precisely when they have become detached from a professional identity defined by others.

- Careers have no reality apart from personal participation in them. Judging success in a career can only come from the perspective of your future integrity.

- Focus is on the task, not the reward. Truth from experience guides expansion of self-created career roles.

- Celebration of self, vocational power, authenticity, integrity, and even sanctity.

Stage Nine: Expansion of Self-Created Roles

- Learns that working is a form of self-expression limited only by the demands of justice, harmony, and mutuality.

- Not owned by career. Truly focused on task, not the reward.

- Begins to love the self they are and the self they want to give the world.

- Learns the magic of believing, going with the flow, the harmony of the universe.

- Major problem: *What is* always has the edge on *what might be*. Easier to settle for reality than truth.

- Joy of doing, of accomplishing, of trying and achieving, is always active. It is accompanied by the joy of transcending ego boundaries to being and becoming part of something greater than yourself.

- Resisting personal growth means sustaining great losses and living at your own peril.

Attaining Self-Actualization in the Workplace

The work of Abraham Maslow, who in the late 1960s began looking at the self-actualized adult, offers us a model for wholeness and well-being that might finally be realized in the emerging world of work. Both organizations and individuals will benefit from this. Self-actualization is defined in various ways, but there is a solid core of agreement around the following definitions:

- acceptance and expression of the inner core or self

- actualization of latent capacities and potentialities resulting in "full functioning"

- availability of human and personal essence, and

- minimal presence of ill health, neurosis, or diminution of the basic human and personal capacities (Maslow, *Toward a Psychology of Being*, p. 197).

Maslow says that "capacities clamor to be used, and cease their clamor only when they are well used. That is capacities are needs. Not only is it fun to use our capacities, but it is also necessary for growth. The unused skill or capacity or organ can become a disease center or else atrophy or disappear, thus diminishing the person" (p. 201). The pursuit of finding and fulfilling oneself through one's work is thus key to a healthy and spiritual lifestyle. This state of full functioning is similar to the flow identified by Mihaly Csikszentmihalyi. Maslow's focus was on human needs that indicate potentialities within a framework of development and growth. He speaks of five levels of need arranged in hierarchical order. The most basic needs must be relatively well satisfied before the individual is able to function at a higher level. A brief summary of Abraham Maslow's hierarchy of needs follows.

1. **Physiological Needs** include hunger, sex, and thirst as well as the need for sleep, food, sexual relations, and bodily integrity.

2. **Safety Needs** are centered around the requirements of a predictable and orderly world. The individual will attempt to organize the world to provide the greatest degree of safety and predictability.

3. **Belonging Needs** indicate the ability to carry on affectionate relationships with other people and belong to a wider group. The person is able to function well in interpersonal situations.

4. **Esteem Needs** constitute the desire for achievement and competence, for independence and freedom, for reputation and prestige. When the satisfaction of all the lower needs has occurred, the final level will be achieved.

5. **Self-Actualization Needs** are met when the individual reaches full use and exploitation of talents, capacities, and potentialities.

Figure 1.1 Maslow's Hierarchy of Needs

Maslow's focus on the healthy person and his intense investigations of a group of self-actualized people found the following characteristics to be evident in those who have achieved that state:

1. They are realistically oriented.

2. They accept themselves, other people, and the natural world.

3. They have a great deal of spontaneity.

4. They are problem-centered rather than self-centered.

5. They have an air of detachment and a need for privacy.

6. They are autonomous and independent.

7. Their appreciation of people and events is fresh rather than stereotyped.

8. Most have had profound mystical or spiritual experiences (not necessarily religious).

9. They identify with mankind.

10. Intimate relationships with a few specially loved people tend to be profound.

11. Their values and attitudes are democratic.

12. They do not confuse means with ends.

13. Their sense of humor is philosophical rather than hostile.

14. They have a great fund of creativeness.

15. They resist conformity to the culture.

16. They transcend the environment rather than just coping with it.

This list of characteristics might fit every employer's profile of the ideal candidate or serve as a working goal for the self-employed person. Working at this level of self-actualization would surely result in more pleasure, harmony, and peace.

Which of Maslow's identified needs are currently being met through your work life? Where are you in your overall personal assessment? Check the characteristics of self-actualized individuals and see which ones you manifest. As you proceed with the process presented in Part Two and reflect on your life work, you may become more aware of times when you reflected these criteria.

Personal Healing and Energy Centers

In order to further focus our attention on understanding how to realize a healthy and spiritual lifestyle through one's work, we turn to the work of Carolyn Myss. In her brilliant works, *Why People Don't Heal and How They Can* and *Anatomy of the Spirit*, she has reinvented an astonishing and insightful model that integrates the chakra system of the Hindus with the Judaic Tree of Life and the Christian sacraments. The concept of understanding that our "biology is our biography" is especially applicable to healing the wounds received from the workplace. You may experience some of the physical symptoms or feel drawn to the feeling state contained in the various chakras as you go through your healing process using this model. As you tell your story through the process of reviewing your life work, you will begin to experience a deeper level of healing resulting in more peace and serenity.

The seven chakras can best be thought of as energy centers connecting the body and the spirit. Like a computer disc, these energy centers are imprinted with information and energy needed by your physical/spiritual body to perform your life work. By familiarizing yourself with the energy system reflected in each of the chakras, you can acquire the grounding needed to be fully present to yourself and today's marketplace. For more information go to her website at http://myss.com.

Here is a brief description of some of the belief patterns and emotions associated with each of the chakras, in ascending order. The mental/emotional issues associated with each chakra activate the chakras' energies and spiritual lessons in sequence from bottom to top. We have also correlated this information with Maslow's needs to help you identify where you are emotionally and spiritually in your own personal journey to discover right livelihood.

First Chakra

This energy center contains the belief patterns most strongly connected to our biological family and our early social environment. Thus this *tribal* energy shows up in concern for safety and security. It is connected to how we relate to the physical world and our ability to provide for life's necessities and stand up for ourselves. The degree to which we are at home with our bodies is the degree to which we are grounded—a major requirement for conducting our work in the world. The affirmation associated with this chakra: **All Is One. Key Word: Tribe.** This stage is associated with the physical needs identified by Maslow.

Figure 1.2 The Human Energy System

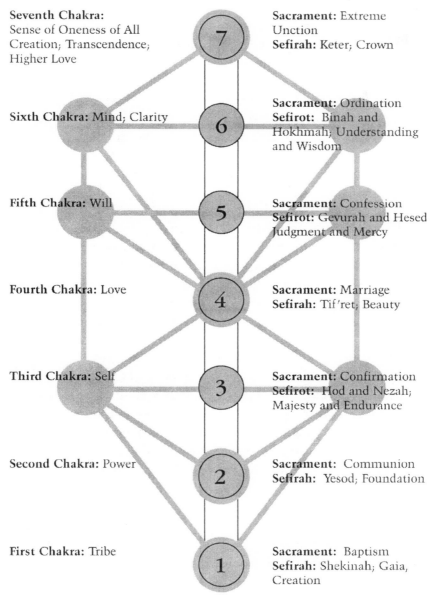

Seventh Chakra: Sense of Oneness of All Creation; Transcendence; Higher Love

Sacrament: Extreme Unction
Sefirah: Keter; Crown

Sixth Chakra: Mind; Clarity

Sacrament: Ordination
Sefirot: Binah and Hokhmah; Understanding and Wisdom

Fifth Chakra: Will

Sacrament: Confession
Sefirot: Gevurah and Hesed Judgment and Mercy

Fourth Chakra: Love

Sacrament: Marriage
Sefirah: Tif'ret; Beauty

Third Chakra: Self

Sacrament: Confirmation
Sefirot: Hod and Nezah; Majesty and Endurance

Second Chakra: Power

Sacrament: Communion
Sefirah: Yesod; Foundation

First Chakra: Tribe

Sacrament: Baptism
Sefirah: Shekinah; Gaia, Creation

The Human Energy System: Correspondences (From *Why People Don't Heal and How They Can* by Carolyn Myss. Copyright © 1997 by Carolyn Myss. Reprinted by the permission of Harmony Books, a division of Crown Publishers.)

Second Chakra

From group control we move to one-on-one relationships, such as friendships, business and financial partnerships, and the use of power. Negative relationships that arise around issues of blame and guilt, money and sex, and power and control inevitably must be resolved. But this is also the seat of creativity, and the development of ethics and honor in all our relationships. The affirmation associated with this chakra: **Honor Others. Key Word: Power.** The safety needs identified by Maslow are met by honoring self and others, and thus include the second and third chakra development.

Third Chakra

This energy center relates to the belief patterns we hold about ourselves. It is the center of our self-esteem and is concerned with issues of trust, care of oneself and others, being responsible for our decisions, and experiencing personal honor. Self-confidence and self-respect are generated at this level as the ego matures. The affirmation associated with this chakra: **Honor Self. Key Word: Self.**

Fourth Chakra

This heart chakra serves to connect the lower three chakras (the tribal energies) with the upper three (the individual and symbolic energies) and has the power to create or destroy. The issues associated with this chakra include love and hatred, resentment and bitterness, and grief and anger. The healing that must take place from the wounds received in today's world of work will be addressed as people deal with the issues of loneliness and commitment, forgiveness and compassion, and ultimately, hope and trust. The affirmation associated with this chakra: **Loving Is Being. Key Word: Love.** This chakra represents the belonging needs identified by Maslow that will be addressed through our interactions with others.

Fifth Chakra

This is the center of willpower, where we make choices and personal commitments and learn to speak our truth. It has to do with finding your voice and following your dream. The energy of this chakra helps you to use personal power to create and learn the important issues of self-control, rather than control over others. The affirmation associated with this chakra: **Surrender to God. Key Word: Will.** The esteem needs identified by Maslow are met through developing the appropriate use of personal power to create an authentic life and are mirrored in the fifth and sixth chakras.

Sixth Chakra

This energy center runs the power of the mind and thus carries tremendous authority. By developing insight and intuition, we learn to see beyond the visible and are empowered to reconsider our beliefs. The pursuit of truth and the ability to be self-reflective enhances our openness to the ideas of others and encourages us to learn from experience. The affirmation associated with this chakra: **Seek the Truth. Key Words: Mind, Clarity.**

Seventh Chakra

The energy of this chakra is like a magnet that draws us upward into divine perception. It is the connector with our spiritual consciousness that urges us to trust life and see our lives in the context of a larger pattern. This chakra encourages us to live a life of values, ethics, courage, and humanitarianism. It generates the transforming spiritual quests and questions such as: Why was I born? What is the deeper meaning of my life? Manifesting the energies of this chakra comes through development of one's faith and spiritual awareness. The affirmation associated with this chakra: **Presence. Key Word: Oneness/Transcendence.** Our self-actualization needs are met when we are doing the work we love and love the way we are doing it. Use the review in Box 1.1 to assess your current energy pattern.

BOX 1.1
Energy System Review

Use the following questionnaire to understand and identify work-related issues associated with the chakras. If, according to Myss, "our biology is our biography," how might the wisdom of the chakra system be used when we are stuck or constricted by a particular life work situation? How do the chakras interplay with the body and the emotions? For more information on how to increase greater self-awareness and bodymindfullness, see "Bodymind" by Ken Dychtwald. Discover how your energy may be blocked. Consider some of the suggestions listed below for moving the energy.

First Chakra Affirmation: All Is One. Keyword: Tribe.

1. What activities make you feel most grounded? Think of a time in your life when you were really present and describe what was going on. Where is your body's energy now while you are reading this book? Do you feel connected to the earth/ground? This lowest chakra reflects survival needs and material concerns, and when blocked can result in a holding on to feelings and a lack of spontaneity.

Second Chakra Affirmation: Honor Others. Keyword: Power.

2. Think of a situation when you felt fully empowered with and by another. Describe what was going on. Who was the person? What was the nature of the relationship? What did you create together? This chakra relates to issues of separation versus openness in our relations to others. Is there a relationship in your life work now that contains issues that need resolving? How can you approach it with new insight?

Third Chakra Affirmation: Honor Self. Keyword: Self.

3. Do you, as a rule, take responsibility for your actions and decisions? Is this true in all areas of your life and business—for example, health-related concerns, recycling waste products, honoring professional commitments (no matter how overloaded you are), and being available with your truest self? You may discover as you go through the process outlined in chapter two, Finding Your True North, something you will be able to commit to in order to honor your self. This third chakra relates to basic issues of control and consumption. How are you feeding and nurturing yourself?

Fourth Chakra Affirmation: Loving Is Being. Keyword: Love.

4. Are you carrying wounds from the workplace that need to be healed in order to continue this journey? Is there anger, bitterness, and/or disappointment holding you back? Can you feel your heart opening to new opportunities to connect with others and begin anew? Acknowledge the loss and prepare to move on to a new beginning. The heart chakra must be both open and properly protected as a channel that lets love flow in and out.

Fifth Chakra Affirmation: Surrender to God. Keyword: Will.

5. By surrendering to what is, we are able to take appropriate action. By being present in the moment, we are able to bring our future into being. What is in your future now? The throat chakra allows you to communicate with thought and feeling, by saying "I am." What choices are you making on a daily basis that allow your authentic self to be present to all that is in your life? A deeper understanding of self stirs and drives spiritual awakening.

Sixth Chakra Affirmation: Seek the Truth. Keyword: Mind, Clarity.

6. As you begin a new project, or approach it on a daily basis, do you remember to center your energy and allow your intuition to be your guide? Are you able to surrender to the outcome, rather than control what is happening? When you face disappointments, are you able to learn from your mistakes? This sixth chakra is known as the third eye and, for many, correlates with what is known as our sixth sense. It involves a higher form of self-awareness that excludes overintellectualizing. The ultimate result is being more interconnected with the larger world.

Seventh Chakra Affirmation: Presence. Keyword: Oneness/Transcendence.

7. In order to further your healing from wounds received in the workplace (or life, for that matter), learn to rely on the spiritual beliefs that speak to you personally. Do you trust life and are you able to see your life in the context of a larger pattern? Are you living your life on purpose and fulfilling your destiny? How do you know that? If you are not, visit the chakra center that needs your attention. At the crown chakra, your full potential is tapped. Tensions dissolve, and unity and transcendence are experienced.

Remember there is a progressive nature and necessity as we follow the energy of the chakras (much like Maslow's hierarchy of needs). You can't jump straight to the top but have to move up the ladder of consciousness and development. The chakras hold challenging patterns of energy along the path toward self-realization that can be activated through meditation and other practices.

By aligning these two models—one of meeting basic needs and the other of personal healing—we can arrive at a fully functioning, healthy place in earning our livelihood. The outcome of self-actualization can be met through discovering one's life work, and the experience of oneness, or transcendence, can be practiced through our daily work routine. Whether you are in the process of discovering your life work or developing mastery in your current area, these models serve as a guide map for achieving and healing. Likewise, when you are feeling stuck, confused, or lack of motivation, it can be a good idea to review these models to determine the challenges you are facing. This process of review and reflection is essential if we hope to continue our active, creative involvement in the world of work.

Getting Started

A final review of the nine stages of career development with the three stages of transition will help you determine your readiness to undertake the career life work process presented in chapter two. If you have recently experienced a loss, or you are finally realizing you have to change your work, you will be working through the issues associated with the first two of the nine stages of career development. Your previous reliance on an absolute authority has been challenged, and the realization that wrong choices are possible may have begun. By opening yourself to trusting in a process, such as the one offered in this book, you will discover greater clarity and experience profound personal growth.

The neutral zone, that murky confusing area where everything is in change and nothing is constant, can be tempered and become richly rewarding if you are fully engaged in this process of finding your true north. This process becomes the authority as you increase your self-awareness and become aware of your ability to make good decisions and implement them. You in fact become the authority in your life by going through stages three, four, five, and six as you realize there may be multiple good options and that you are in charge of your choices.

And finally, having gathered all the information about yourself and having targeted and negotiated your place in the world of work that this process requires, you will be ready for your new beginning. As career becomes a form of self-identity and self-expression, one is able to assume personal responsibility for the good and bad that inevitably occur. One is truly focused on the task more than the rewards, and experiences the joy of doing and accomplishing while being part of something greater than one's self.

This journey toward meaningful life work is the journey of self-actualization and personal healing. Finding "your true gladness" and matching it with "the world's deep hunger" can be realized through the process in chapter two: Finding Your True North. We welcome you now to begin the journey of discovering your meaningful work.

Websites Referenced

global:ideas:bank
www.globalideasbank.org

Dan Pink
www.danpink.com/

Caroline Myss
www.myss.com

2

Finding Your True North: Creating a Life Work Objective

There is a revolution in values taking place among many workers today who are being affected by changes in the world of work. Some are being dispossessed or disempowered while others are experiencing profound opportunity. Many are feeling betrayed by the workplace, but the truth of the matter is, their own values contributed to keeping that illusion alive. The economic and global forces are such now that no matter what, all must create a new reality for themselves in relation to earning a livelihood.

In the twenty-first century, many more people will be making work-related, economic, and survival choices by going within to discover their "deep gladness." Once that unique form of self-expression is defined, and the "hungry places" in the universe identified, the marketplace will begin to be transformed. An important belief that is influencing the creation of this new reality is the ancient truth spoken in *Hamlet*: "To thine own self be true, and it must follow as the night the day, Thou cans't not then be false to any other man." But in order for that to occur in the world at large, we need to realize the fulfillment of another ancient truth, a truth that exists in every culture throughout the world: "Do unto others as you would have others do unto you." The reestablishment of that value, known as the Golden Rule, as a cornerstone of the twenty-first century world of work, may ensure our survival. By fully realizing your potential, you will be putting your spirit to work in ways that are rewarding, fulfilling, and transforming of yourself and the workplace.

The journey of discovery of self and place in the world is ever-changing, ever-renewing, and ever-revitalizing. Whether you choose to stay with the same field to achieve career mastery, change fields, or focus on another sector of life, such as community service, personal growth, or family, the steps in the journey are the same. The journey includes: creating self-awareness through reflection and observation; discerning emerging and changing wants, needs, and interests; prioritizing and decision making; exploring opportunities; connecting with the new; deepening of meaning; and recycling to self-awareness again.

The Career and Life Work Process for Mastering Change

Figure 2.1 Mastering Life Work Transitions

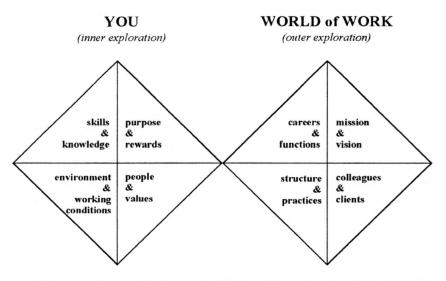

The two diamond shapes in Figure 2.1 represent the processes of inner and outer exploration, which are best approached consecutively. The inner exploration you will undergo gives definition to that which is unique in you; the outer exploration is your search for ideal opportunities in the marketplace. The diamond shape represents the expanding knowledge that comes from gathering the information and then prioritizing (narrowing) the most essential. Richard Bolles stresses the importance of prioritizing when he says, "No exercise is complete until it has been prioritized." Over the years we have met with many people suffering from information overload; what they needed was help separating the essential from the nonessential in order to create focused objectives and move efficiently into the outer diamond, to explore the world of work.

Self-Assessment

The first diamond represents the self-assessment process (chapter two, steps 1 through 5) through which you identify the important criteria for creating your personal mandala and life work objective. This assessment model guides you in answering four key questions to arrive at the core criteria that will define your functioning in a self-actualized state through your work.

The upper left quadrant emphasizes the assessment of **what** you like to do and do well. The assessment helps you find your language and voice as a means of self-expression. It represents your competencies, areas of interest and expertise, functional skills, and special knowledge that will provide focus into work worth doing.

Figure 2.2   Finding Your True North

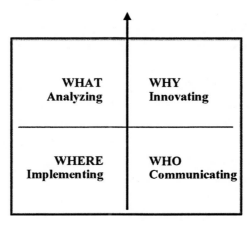

The lower left quadrant has you gather and record information about **where** you have done and would like to do your best work. This focuses your awareness on the structure, environment, and setting where you have done your best work. Here you can also define lifestyle issues, especially as they relate to earning and thriving in the new millennium. The lower right quadrant helps you focus on **who** you enjoy working and creating with, especially the kinds of people and the characteristics that define your best "people setting." When people experience congruency between their personal values and those of colleagues, or their organization's mission, they will be most satisfied. The upper right quadrant focuses your attention on **why** you do what you do, the rewards, the highest values and aspirations you hope to fulfill. It is in this quadrant that you assess what is required to feel fulfilled, to experience meaning and purpose, to know that what you are doing indeed makes a difference.

As you learn to function from your core, you will be actualizing each of the four areas as you realize that the whole is greater than the sum of the parts. Experiencing self-actualization can be a result of doing what you love in the perfect environment with the most fascinating people, making a contribution, and feeling fulfilled in your deepest values and rewards. Abraham Maslow in his work *Religious Values and Peak Experiences* speaks of those people who are "non-peakers" as being exclusively means-oriented, because peak experiences "earn no money, bake no bread, and chop no wood." In the context of finding and creating meaningful work, where the means and the end must be congruent, peak experiences are not only possible, but become more plausible as a result of going through this process.

As you learn to master this process, you will find you can use it again and again to assess any work situation. If you discover one aspect of your work that is out of focus, you can begin to strategize what you can do to bring yourself back to center. Often it is helpful to realize what is out of sync; for example, if you are working on a project with people you really dislike, won't it be helpful to know that and address the issues rather than remain upset? As a result, you are able to get on with the project and bring it to completion harmoniously. Later you can review that experience and clarify the lessons to determine new criteria to incorporate into your ever-evolving and more fully refined personal objective.

This four-part method of questioning and reviewing is at the heart of this process of clarifying and staying centered in your personal mandala, which will result in the creation of several life work objectives. The process will deepen your spiritual understanding through increased conscious awareness of self in relation to others (your community) and to your work (your purpose). The process can be used to delineate a career path as well as redefine a lifestyle, such as planning for retirement. It can also be used to spiritualize your daily journey as you follow this path of self-actualization. See the Spiritual Autobiography exercise in step 1 if you wish to undertake this process as a spiritual journey. And finally, going through this process of career and life work exploration can heal the wounded places in our physical, mental/emotional, and spiritual lives.

To achieve career mastery the four key questions of **What, Where, Who,** and **Why** will need to be answered at four different levels:

1. to clarify and define your individual profile

2. to create objectives and verify your interests

3. to explore and narrow a specific path or vocation

4. to determine that you are uniquely qualified to fulfill this opportunity

Your goal throughout the process is to maximize the match and the fit between all four quadrants on the inner and outer levels of exploration. Once the internal assessment is solidly completed, you can begin the external exploration that will allow you to identify and select the criteria you have identified and prioritize so that you can compromise when needed. In this way, you increase your individual sense of personal power and choice in the workplace.

Exploring the World of Work

The exploration into the world of work begins by seeking the best match between the many facets of your personal mandala and a multitude of employment opportunities. In chapter three we have identified a seven-step process for researching career and employment opportunities using some wonderful Internet sites that provide valuable information on your areas of interest. Once you have identified your criteria, you can focus your research on a specific employment objective using these tools and social media. While employing the job search strategies and researching the Internet, you will be gathering new thoughts and insights to validate the information you have gathered about yourself and what you need to feel challenged and stay committed. Your self-awareness will deepen as you gain confidence from making the choices and commitments that each stage of exploration requires. Your intention will become clearer as you explore opportunities and make connections with others that provide additional clarification. Your commitment to yourself will deepen as you adhere to the process of constantly referring to this inner/outer exploration to define where you are on your journey. If you are spiritually attuned, you will come to realize that some deeper truths become evident, thereby making the journey even more mystical and rewarding.

If you will visualize the job search process–or the process of prospecting using the following four-part model and asking similar questions, you will have a solid means for exploring new opportunities. Visiting the upper left quadrant in the second diamond, you will now be concerned with identifying the different career areas and functional areas that best reflect your prioritized skills and knowledge sets. By asking the questions "**What** are the different career areas and **what** are the functional areas that match my interests?" you begin the external career exploration process. After identifying the appropriate fields or industries, you continue your exploration by exploring the important question: "**What** needs doing in that world?" Remember that this is the key question to finding work that needs doing. And if you are the one to define it, who better to answer the question, demonstrate the necessary skills and knowledge, interests, and values that will position you as the primary resource? Using the powerful tool of the Internet, you can research all the issues relevant to your focus and gather precise information about the current state of the art in relation to that specific concern.

Information from your individual self-assessment and the results from other career interest inventories will provide you with the criteria you need to identify the environment, structure, and workplace setting, as well as the people and value factors that will best match your profile. You will be verifying "**Where** will my work style fit and **who** are the people I will be working with and serving?" The more information you have about your wants and needs, the easier it will be to gather information about various settings. It will also enable you to accept a compromise that is acceptable to and defined by you.

The final area of match that needs to be met is in the area of individual purpose and organizational purpose and mission. "**Why** do organizations exist?" is geared toward helping you assess the mission and value system of the organization to which you are attracted. The following definitions are taken from "Purpose, Mission, and Vision," *The New Paradigm in Business.*

Purpose is seen as "the fundamental set of reasons for the organization's existence; purpose is something that is always worked towards, but never fully realized." *Mission* is defined as "a clear, definable and motivational point of focus—an achievable goal, a finish line to work towards." There can be a lot of confusion around mission and purpose. "Because a specific mission can be so compelling, many organizations make the mistake of thinking that their mission is their fundamental purpose. The problem becomes: what do you do once you've fulfilled the mission? Without a broader, more creative purpose from which to derive the next mission, there will be a crisis of direction once the mission is accomplished." This issue likewise becomes true for the individual in relation to personal goal setting and overall purpose. The action steps resulting from goal setting become the measurable activities that will enable you to fulfill your purpose.

And finally, *vision* is defined as the "ability to see the potential or necessity of opportunities right in front of you … it is intuitive … it is knowing 'in your bones' what can or must be done. In other words, vision isn't forecasting the future, it is creating the future by taking action in the present" (*The New Paradigm in Business*, p. 87). As every responsible worker knows, being proactive is key to successfully managing life work transitions, and the development of this kind of vision is a key benefit of completing the assessment process that follows.

When you are able to identify where you are on the journey, by referring to the process and models outlined here, you will find yourself self-actualizing through your work. Are the rewards you are receiving from the universe the ones you want or need? If not, why not? What compromises have you chosen to make to actualize some other aspect of your life? Perhaps an illness requires you to refocus your energy, or achieving a goal ahead of the planned time gives you an opportunity to pick up another passion that will help you feel fulfilled. The process of personal journaling as you go through this exploration process will help you become aware of the serendipitous events in your life now that may provide important clues to your future. Examples in your daily life you may want to record include writing about the satisfaction felt in knowing beyond a shadow of a doubt you have done your best work. Or, you may choose to write about a changing relationship with a coworker in order to heighten your awareness of your deep connection with another. This level of conscious processing using a personal journal will deepen your sense of connectedness, wonder, and awe as you go through this process.

Discovering Your Life Work Objective

Beginning with step 1 you will be asked to tell your story. There are several exercises here to begin your self-assessment. The key to each of them is to allow yourself to gain insight into how you would answer the four key questions in a comprehensive and/or historical review of your life. For example, you can analyze each work experience using the simple formula: **What** was I doing? Then evaluate it. Did I like it or not? **Where** was I doing it? What did I like about that or not? **Who** was I doing it with and for? And **how** did I feel about that? And last, but not least, **Why** was I doing it? What were the expected rewards? What was unexpected? Did I feel fulfilled?

We have also included in step 1 summaries of several major career assessment and interest inventories. We carefully preselected the Internet sites and assessment tools that will provide you with the most accurate, vital, and helpful information for identifying and verifying actual career objectives and functional areas. We have included the Myers Briggs Type Indicator (MBTI), because of its universal appeal to people going through change. The relationship of career areas to type in MBTI language provides an excellent starting point for career exploration. John Holland's Career Game is also recommended to augment the process if you want additional clarification.

What Do I Love and Do Best?

In step 2, Defining Core Competencies, you will begin the systematic analysis of what you most enjoy doing. This is the rich upper left quadrant, where your knowledge and the value you add to the workplace is defined. Through the process of identifying skills, knowledge, and adaptive skills directly from your life story, you will become profoundly aware of your unique talents and resources. Using our skills inventory will help you organize your functional skills into multiple skill sets that can be used in a variety of settings. The process of prioritizing and sorting skills dramatically increases your marketability and your self-awareness about the transferability of your multiple skill sets. A thorough assessment of your skills and knowledge would not be complete without the opportunity to develop a plan for continuous learning. To remain a vital contributor in your chosen area, it is necessary to be self-directed and motivated. You will also have the opportunity to assess the career management and self-employment competencies mentioned as key to successful employability.

Defining and Clarifying Personal Criteria

Step 3, Redefining Your Self: Passions, Preferences, and Purpose, offers many different exercises for getting at the core values you need to have met to self-actualize through your work. The criteria generated from these exercises, as well as the interest inventories on the

Internet, offer rich information for further defining yourself. Some of the information will help you to define the ideal kind of working conditions, the environment, even the structure of work as defined by the new employment contract. People who want more security than others may need to honor that value and seek out one single employer who can perhaps meet that need, in spite of the trend toward multiple employment opportunities. Other criteria will be used to identify the characteristics and traits of the kinds of people with whom you wish to associate.

Individuals need first and foremost to experience congruency between their personal value systems and that of the organization or individuals with whom they affiliate. When there is an internal value conflict, it must be resolved in order to continue. Knowing your own values will help you distinguish between internal and external value conflicts. So often, difficulties at work occur because of difficulties in getting along with others. Because the new workplace calls for enhanced interpersonal, facilitation, and community technology-building skills, we can only hope that when value conflicts arise, they will be better managed. Still, when you are cocreating and collaborating with a partner who makes your heart sing, what could be better? Defining your ideal people criteria will help you recognize them when you see them.

In addition to identifying criteria for filling in the where and who areas of this model, this chapter also helps you get clear on why you do what you do. It helps you identify core values that when fulfilled increase your sense of self-esteem. It helps you identify your personal purpose that can give meaning and direction to your entire life or can become the major focus of your life work. For those people who want to make a difference, the fulfillment of this criterion will be most important.

Creating Balance and Wholeness through Goal Setting

The next to final piece of self-assessment (step 4) consists of goal setting and further visualizations around what you need to feel fulfilled and rewarded. This step allows you to begin to look at other areas of your life and see what you need to do to increase value in areas such as personal relationships, leisure activities, spiritual practice, health and wellness, and learning. By creating a sense of the whole that is balanced, it is easier to focus on those areas that are most out of alignment. You will be able to regulate your energies and achieve what is most important overall, by defining what is "enough" in terms of activity and finances. To develop a career action plan without looking at the rest of your life would be a serious error in your goal for finding fulfillment through work. Not to mention the fact that the important task of managing your career requires a great deal of focus and determination, so you must be vigilant overall in how you spend your time.

All of the exercises are listed on the www.lifeworktransitions. com website for your convenience. The directions for completing each exercise can be found here in the text.

Pulling Together Your Profile: A Mandala for Success

As mentioned earlier, the admonishment that "no exercise is complete until it has been prioritized" will now receive your full attention. Each exercise that you completed requires some kind of assessment and delineation of the criteria that are most important to you. In step 5 you will once again review all the information and create a visual profile to summarize it and create a personal mandala. Shifting from the more analytical and linear process of gathering and recording information, I invite you now to move into your creative self and develop a visual representation of all you have discovered. This time you will be prioritizing the information with the intention of realizing your next steps leading toward the fulfillment of your life work goals. You will also be guided through a detailed process for translating your unique profile into several life work objectives to conduct your search into the world of work. The process of career and life work mastery offers continual renewal and commitment to that which is highest and most true within us and our genuine desire to make a difference. The journey to discover the truth within is, for the most part, an inner search.

> The longest journey
> is the journey inwards
>   of him who has chosen his destiny

who has started upon his quest
for the source of his being.
Dag Hammerskold

The journey to finding your right livelihood requires action and reflection, extension of effort, surrender to what is, and mastering the high-tech/high-touch tools included here. Let the journey begin.

Figure 2.3 You in the World of Work

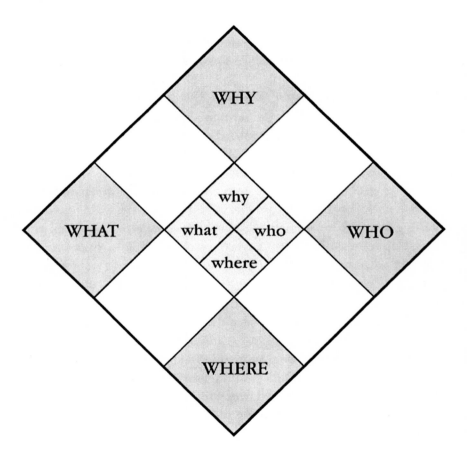

STEP #1

Telling Your Story

To know where you are going, you must know where you have been. —*David Campbell*

Telling your story is at the heart of this process. It is both time-consuming and fulfilling. You will get out of it exactly what you put into it. The initial selection of the most appropriate exercise for you sets the stage for the unfolding to follow. By authoring your own story, you begin to acquire the perspective that you have indeed authored your life. Henri Nouwen, in his book *Reaching Out*, asks the following questions to underscore the value of this approach: "What if the events of our history are molding us as a sculptor molds his clay, and if it is only in a careful obedience to these molding hands that we can discover our real vocation and become mature people? What if our history does not prove to be a blind impersonal sequence of events over which we have no control, but rather reveals to us a guiding hand pointing to a personal encounter in which all our hopes and aspirations will reach their fulfillment?"

You will discover in writing your story that even in those circumstances under which you felt you had little or no control, you always had choices of how to respond. By reviewing your past with compassion and the intention of increasing understanding and personal insight, you will be able to rewrite the script. And finally, you will begin to be in charge of your own choices as you learn to accept personal responsibility for what has been. The key to answering the question "Who am I, at my core?" means finding the essence of spirit within your life's experiences. The answers are found through reviewing and exploring work experiences, accomplishments, and personal history. By naming our life experience, we can give meaning and value to our life choices. Thus, our sense of personal power is enhanced, and we can let go of any sense of victim mentality, self-pity, or even personal aggrandizement. What remains is a clear strong sense of personal accomplishments, skills, and wonderfully rich information about the pleasures and rewards from work that you find meaningful. More specifically, we can often heal the wounds inflicted by dysfunctional workplaces by reviewing the past and telling our stories.

Through any of the self-assessment exercises included in step 1, you will begin the process of uncovering clues to your personal life work objective. These exercises provide you with the opportunity to get in touch with positive emotions experienced at better times in your life that will result in higher energy levels and greater self-esteem. By immersing yourself in the process, by selecting an exercise and beginning to tell your story, you will immediately experience an improved sense of well-being. And finally, telling your story using your own language raises your consciousness to better describe yourself. The process of expanding your vocabulary is also crucial to your resume preparation and preparation for interviewing. Telling your story often reveals what you might perceive as an insignificant, or seemingly irrelevant, experience that "you just loved" and that may provide clues to discovering what will make you happy in the future. Using our four-part model for analysis, ask yourself:

- **Why** did you love the experience?

- **What** were you doing, **who** were you with, **what** kind of **support** and **energy** were exchanged?

- **What** kind of **rewards** were you receiving?

- And finally, **what else** was going on in your life at the time, or after hours?

The exercises that follow will help you get in touch with skills, values, preferences, interests, and directions that will be sorted and prioritized throughout this process. When a client lights up with a smile while telling her story, I know we are on to something. Other clues that suggest you have hit "gold" may include feeling a burst of energy, or the articulation of such phrases as "I loved that job," "it was my favorite," or "the best thing that ever happened to me." Even people who are in the midst of a very dark phase when undertaking this self-assessment can usually experience some kind of positive awareness. If you have difficulty getting started, think about asking a close friend or loved one to help you by brainstorming activities or experiences where they knew you were really at your personal best. The emphasis throughout this process is to focus on the positive at the exclusion of the negative, so it will be important for you to generate enough positive experiences to continue the self-assessment phase. With over seven different recommended exercises in this step you are sure to find one that works for you.

Selecting the Exercise

The four written exercises are designed to elicit your own form of creative self-expression and reflect your personal circumstances. These exercises have been staples in our counseling for years, and their worth has passed the test of time with positive results. You are invited to select one or more that best suits your style. Whichever exercise you select, try to follow the guidelines presented, but use your own imagination. If you think of a way to tell your story that works better for you, by all means go right ahead. This is your story, and it provides valuable clues to your future. Tell it the way it really was; brag a little, brag a lot. Treat yourself to the love and appreciation that may have been lacking from peer and supervisor reviews. No politics here. You are free to tell your story as you experienced it.

Types of Exercises

Listed here are the four types of written exercises that can be prepared, with brief definitions, and some pros and cons of why you might prefer one approach over the other. For specific directions for each of the exercises, turn to the end of the step or go to the exercise section at our website www.lifeworktransitions.com. It is recommended that you complete one of these exercises before going on to the next section.

Life Work Autobiography: Telling Your Story

Writing your life work autobiography provides valuable insight into your life as a whole and your work in particular. As a result, you will better understand the transitions from one job to the next and the choices you made at different stages in your career. The specifics of each work segment will be analyzed further in subsequent steps to provide clues for determining your future life work. This comprehensive review will provide many valuable insights.

Accomplishments Inventory

Creating an inventory of accomplishments that were enjoyable and meaningful inside and outside of work can also provide important information. By naming accomplishments from your past and their relative value, you will be able to determine which values still hold meaning for you. This approach will also help you understand experientially why some values are more important to you than others. This exercise is helpful if you have not enjoyed your career thus far, are just starting out, or have a lifetime of volunteer experience you want to carry into the workplace.

An *accomplishment* is anything you did well, enjoyed, and took some action to achieve. Your accomplishments are things you have done at home, in a part-time or full-time job, or in your hobbies or volunteer activities. An accomplishment does *not* mean something you do better than anyone else; it only means something you learned to do and that once you could not do, for example, "I achieved the goal of the fund-raising drive." We often encourage clients to conduct this inventory from their earliest memories up until their first job, so they can realize the importance and influence of their formative experiences. Or, if you've liked some of your work, but feel it doesn't express all of you, use a combination of these first two exercises.

Drawing Your Life Line

If you are a visual-spatial person who doesn't like to write, then the life-line exercise of drawing your life journey and using visual symbols/metaphors will work for you. It does not mean you have to consider yourself artistic or creative. Often working in a medium with which you are not familiar will allow your creativity to come forth. Another advantage of this exercise is that it gives you the opportunity to see your life as a series of events unfolding in the journey of your life. It offers the added advantage of being able to add details at a later date if you forget them and then ask yourself, "Why did I leave that out the first time? It was so important." For people who don't know where to begin but feel their life as a whole is a story worth telling, this is a good place to begin. It is also considered the first step in preparing to write the spiritual autobiography.

Spiritual Autobiography: Finding Your Voice

If you want to look at your life from a spiritual perspective, then the spiritual autobiography will be the best place for you to begin this process. The purpose of this exercise is to reveal the underlying pattern of your life experiences and help you "uncover the potential within the acorn," as James Hillman said in *The Soul's Code.* This will help you discover your unique perspective and expression. In this exercise you will be looking for meaningful experiences, the turning points, the triumphs and crashes, the "dark night of the soul" experiences where all of your talents and gifts came into being.

For many people undergoing midlife changes, this exercise will take you on a wonderful journey of discovery and self-awareness. This journey is for the most part an inner search, and it calls you to live inside the difficult questions, such as "Why am I here?" and "What is my reason for being?" If you are plagued by these questions, consider the advice of the great poet and mystic Rilke. "Be patient toward all that is unsolved in your heart and try to love the questions themselves." Living inside the questions means living with tension. Many of us may have a vision and a desire to know what we can contribute or how we might make a difference. But in addition to living with the questions, you must also accept the responsibility that for some time, your purpose may be to discover your purpose. How you will fulfill that may be illusive and mysterious. This exercise provides the framework for exploration.

Some of the insights people have as a result of these exercises can yield a great deal of perspective on their current situations. These realizations become evident by examining objectively the previous events of our lives. Such awareness might include the following observations: "I see that every positive experience I had was followed by a real down" or "negative experiences always involved too much contact with people." These natural tendencies or patterns, and we all have them, can be indicators to us—if only we will pay attention to them—of what motivates us and brings out our best. These insights are the building blocks of your new definition.

Self-Assessment Instruments on the Internet

There are several assessment instruments on the Internet that will help you understand yourself as the author of your story and provide indicators of your interests. Many career consultants rely heavily on their results. With our emphasis on having you tell your personal story first, the results of these self-assessment instruments will hopefully reinforce your self-definition as they provide vital clues that will connect you to the world of work. They will be useful in verifying your interests and targeting different occupational areas.

Myers-Briggs Type Indicator

Another instrument that we feel is of great value is the Myers-Briggs Type Indicator (MBTI). The instrument provides a great deal of insight into your preferred style of working and being. A modified, yet highly reliable version of the instrument can be found at http://www.humanmetrics.com/cgi-win/JTypes2.asp.

This instrument is extremely valid and widely used by many organizations to focus on strengths of contributing team members. The model created by Kathryn Myers and Isabel Briggs Myers draws heavily on the research of Carl Jung, the great depth psychologist. The model represents your preferences on four scales. Preferences indicate an ease in style and approach. These characteristics are strong indicators of your preferred working style. Your preferences are indicated on a continuum of opposites. Extroverts

(E) tend to focus on the outer world of people and things and are energized by that outer world. They tend to "think out loud" and are more action oriented than the Introverts (I). Introverts prefer to focus on the inner world of thoughts and ideas. They prefer to understand the world before experiencing it, so they often "think first, then act."

The next two scales represent the functions of Sensing (S) and Intuiting (N), and Thinking (T) and Feeling (F) as defined by Jung. These four functions have the most to do with career satisfaction and match our four-part model for assessment. The Sensing (S) and Intuiting (N) functions describe how you prefer to take in information. The Sensing (S) person tends to use the five senses to take in information about the world and sees it in a detailed, practical, sequential manner. Intuiting (N) people tend to overlook the details, and instead look for a pattern, possibilities, or meaning. Intuiting people use their imagination to see what might be, rather than what is. In our model, Sensing (S) people may be most concerned with their environment (the lower left quadrant) and have a preference for maintaining systems and structures. Intuitive people may be more concerned with what could be or what might be, using their imagination to explore why things are the way they are (the upper right quadrant).

The next function has to do with how one makes decisions or uses information. The Thinking (T) person tends to be more analytical, objective, and focused on principles and justice—for example, what is the right thing to do in a situation that makes sense to them? Feeling (F) people, on the other hand, may be more subjective in their decision making and focused on values and creating harmony. The Thinking (T) person is often more prone to give precise, immediate feedback, while the Feeling (F) person will be more appreciative and empathic. In our model, the Thinking (T) function is represented by the upper left quadrant, where objectivity, analysis, and doing the right thing are valued. The Feeling (F) function is represented by awareness of the people with whom we communicate and their values. This decision making is based on harmony; it does not refer to your feelings about the decision and is represented by the lower right quadrant.

The final scale describes the lifestyle you prefer in relating to the outer world. Those who prefer a Judging (J) attitude tend to be organized and enjoy making decisions. They want to regulate their environment and like to get closure on projects and events. Perceiving (P) persons tend to deal with the outer world in a flexible, spontaneous way. They prefer to gather information, keep their options open, and trust themselves to adapt to the moment. Remember, each of the four MBTI preferences indicate work-related preferences and your overall profile will show strong characteristics related to many different occupations. Understanding your type is important; validating the information about your preferences is essential. Trust the results from this instrument and record the results in your personal mandala.

Holland's Career Interest Game

One very useful tool, the **Career Interest Game,** can be accessed on the Internet at www.missouriwestern.edu/careerdevelopment/cig/. It is a fun tool to take, and it will help you identify interests as they match with other vocational indicators you will be uncovering through the self-assessment exercises. After reading the descriptions and selecting the top three areas that best reflect your interests, click on the question mark to get more information. Be sure to highlight the most relevant information to you and keep it handy so that you can refer to it later in step 5 when you begin to bring your profile together.

To match your Myers-Briggs Type Profile with career interests go to http://student.ccbcmd.edu/~hzlotow1/mbti.pdf. From this page you can go directly to the U.S. Department of Labor and review the career listings at www.bls.gov/search/ooh.htm after you have identified your type and selected several careers you'd like to explore.

Exercises

BOX 1.1

Work Autobiography Guidelines

To know where we are going, we must know where we have been. This exercise is designed to help you recreate your life work history in an orderly, organized manner. The important thing is to be as detailed as possible, as though you were describing your experiences to a child. Autobiographies vary in length from fifteen to forty pages. Start off with a chronological list of all your work experiences according to time segments (some people like to include high school and college as their first "work" segments).

Year	Position	Organization	Location
1967–69	Asst. Production Mgr.	Beacon Press, Inc.	Boston
1969–70	Editing, Design	Freelance	Boston

Use this summary as the framework for your detailed autobiography. Describe exactly what you did and accomplished and try to overcome your natural modesty by bragging a bit. Your evaluation is what counts here. In fact, the activities you enjoyed the most deserve the most attention. In describing each segment, be sure to respond to the following points.

1. Describe the organization, its size, general purpose, and so on.

2. Outline your responsibilities, personnel supervised, budget concerns, and amounts of money you handled and/or equipment you handled. What exactly did you do?

---

3. Describe significant achievements, especially those that went particularly well without a great deal of effort on your part. Describe any organizational activities or innovations that made your job easier. Describe any special relations with other people and any personal contributions you made.

4. Describe what was going on after hours—hobbies, activities, organizations, relationships, and so on.

BOX 1.2

Accomplishments Inventory Guidelines

1. Take a separate sheet of paper for every five-year period of your life up to and including your present age. On each sheet, make a list of your accomplishments for that period of time. There should be at least three to five accomplishments for every five-year period. Pick those accomplishments that you most enjoyed doing or the ones that were most satisfying to you in some way. The most useful way to state the accomplishment is by using the "I" statement and an action verb; for example, "I learned how to play the guitar." If you have trouble remembering, just close your eyes and picture yourself actually going through the steps, and answer the question "What was I doing?"

2. Next to each accomplishment you list, state why this was satisfying or meaningful to you. You do not need to write a paragraph; one statement will do.

3. After you have listed the accomplishments, choose the five to seven accomplishments that seem to be most meaningful to you. These may come from any five-year period. Your task now is to define your experiences in as much detail as possible. It is important that you mention every action that you took. Just tell it as though you were telling a story to a child—begin at the beginning and go through to the end.

4. Important points to remember:

    a. Describe how the event started and who started it.

    b. Describe any planning or preparation you did for it.

    c. Familiarize yourself with the Action Word sheet in the resume section. Discuss every detail of the project using action words.

    d. Describe any interactions you had with people involved in the project.

    e. Describe your personal outcome in terms of accomplishments/success/good feelings.

BOX 1.3

Lifeline Exercise Guidelines

Get a large sheet of easel paper or shelf paper. You will need crayons, magic markers, and pens. For fun, you might want to have stickers, feathers, glitter, and other assorted materials, including pictures cut out of magazines or pictures of you at various stages of your life.

Begin by drawing a lifeline that best represents your sense of your life. Is it a straight line, or does it have lots of peaks and valleys? Whatever form your lifeline takes will work. Trust your hand as it draws a basic form that will give shape to the following steps in the exercise. You may want to do this first part in pencil, so if you need to make changes later on you can.

You will most likely want to include some of the major experiences in your life, such as entering first grade or your first summer job. You will also want to list major events such as marriage, children, jobs, and subsequent career life work events. As you recollect each experience and assess its value, your lifeline will visually begin to reflect the highs and the lows. You can use the crayons to draw pictures or symbols or use words and phrases to identify the value you ascribe to it. When done, you will not only have the wonderful feeling of having created a masterpiece that provides a comprehensive overview of your life, but you will also be able to see and interpret patterns that have occurred throughout time.

BOX 1.4
Spiritual Autobiography Guidelines

In order to transform a personal or professional experience into spiritual insight and understanding, it is necessary to gain some perspective. The writing of one's spiritual autobiography can cover your entire life, or you can select several significant experiences and write about them in detail.

Use the Lifeline Exercise to identify the events you might wish to write about. Consider events in your life that were formative to your beliefs. As a child, what were some significant spiritual experiences? Then think of yourself as an adolescent and remember the first time you might have believed something different from your family. Who were some significant role models for you and why? As a young adult, where did you go for spiritual insight? What kind of peak experiences did you have or what kind of community were you seeking? Create an outline of events from the above that you want to explore from a spiritual perspective.

1. Describe the situation and your role. What went particularly well, with a minimum of effort? What special challenges did you overcome? What special talents did you use?

2. What values were met and which were being challenged or threatened?

3. Describe the people involved and your relation to them. Who was there for you? What relations were deepened as a result of the experience? Which spiritual values were expressed and by whom?

4. Finally, write about the gifts you received as a result of this experience. What were the rewards? Did you overcome a weakness or fear, and how has the experience made a difference in your life?

Websites Referenced

Life Work Transitions
www.lifeworktransitions.com

MBTI
www.humanmetrics.com/cgi-win/JTypes2.asp

Career Interest Game
www.missouriwestern.edu/careerdevelopment/cig/

Combination of MBTI & Career Interests
http://student.ccbcmd.edu/~hzlotow1/mbti.pdf

Bureau of Labor Statistics
www.bls.gov/search/ooh.htm

STEP #2

Defining Core Competencies

> Our sense of security in this new age will be found in our toolbox of skills and experiences, in our attitude toward work, in what we contribute, in what we do that is fantastic, in what we do that makes us employable, not in passive dependency on our employer or on a set of unchanging skills. —*Robert Jay Ginn, Jr.*

The new employment contract in the contemporary American workplace requires employees to assemble and manage multiple skill sets that can be arranged in a variety of combinations. The traditional hierarchical workplace providing a lifetime of security has been replaced by a flattened organization promising change. In order to survive in the new workplace, employees have to be prepared for multiple employability options. Implicit in this scenario is the assumption that employees continually add to their skill sets to maintain optimal flexibility in their adaptation to change. Consequently, identifying your skills—those that you have and those that you will need—is essential to your future.

The secretary of the United States Department of Labor established a Secretary's Commission on Achieving Necessary Skills (SCANS) to identify skills required for the workplace of the future. (The SCANS Report can be found at www.academicinnovations.com/report.html.) Other organizations, such as the American Society for Training and Development, the National Academy of Sciences, and Stanford University, have also studied this topic. The results of these studies were similar. SCANS concluded that regardless of job title or position description, employees must be able to demonstrate their skill in managing and using:

1. **Resources**. Workers must be able to identify, organize, plan, and allocate resources such as time, money, materials, and facilities. They must also be able to assess human resources in terms of skills, evaluation, and feedback.

2. **Interpersonal Skills**. Competent employees are those who can work well with team members and can teach new workers; can serve clients directly and persuade coworkers either individually or in groups; can negotiate with others to solve problems or reach decisions; can work comfortably with colleagues from diverse backgrounds; and can responsibly challenge existing procedures and policies.

3. **Information**. Workers need to be able to identify, assimilate, pare, maintain, and interpret quantitative and qualitative records; convert information from one form to another; and convey information, orally and in writing, as the need arises.

4. **Systems**. Workers must understand their own work in the context of the work of those around them; they must understand how parts of systems are connected, anticipate consequences, and monitor and correct their own performance; they must be able to identify trends and anomalies in system performance, integrate multiple displays of data, and link symbols (e.g., displays on a computer screen) with real phenomena (e.g., machine performance).

5. **Technology**. Workers must demonstrate high levels of competence in selecting and using appropriate technology, visualizing operations, using technology to monitor tasks, and maintaining and troubleshooting complex equipment.

How do your skills match up with these? You will know by the end of this step. We have provided a skills inventory that will help you determine and define what you can do and what you enjoy doing. The inventory uses words commonly used in the world of work, which will increase your own vocabulary and help you immensely when you write your resume and sell yourself in an interview.

When you analyze the results of the skills inventory, you will be able to compare your skills with the five SCANS competencies, choose the skills you enjoy most and want to use in the future, and assess your strengths and weaknesses. The identification of weaknesses gives valuable information and will point you toward the training you need to stay competitive in the workplace.

Many clients think they know what their skills are and are somewhat resistant to the exercises in this step. Often we hear, "Well, I know I am a people person." What does that mean? Are you a good speaker in front of a large audience? Are you a very good listener in a one-on-one encounter? Do you like lots of contact with people but not in a personal way? Do you socialize well? Do you like to interview people and then write a story? Do you like to have people around but really work by yourself? Just saying "I'm a people person" doesn't cut it when you are trying to sell yourself in the marketplace. You need to be able to articulate the specific ways you work with and for people.

You will be using information from "Your Story" written in step 1 to discover and refine the definition of skills you most enjoy or want to acquire. This may seem like a tedious task, and it is tempting to quickly look through the list of skills and check off those you think you have. However, if you go through the process outlined in this step, you will discover more than just the skills you think you have. There will be many skills that you haven't thought of in a long time, skills you have taken for granted, or skills you really enjoyed but haven't consciously owned because you used them in nonwork settings. The unexpected insights can play an enormous part in your choices for the future. In addition, the process of owning your skills is one of the most powerful exercises for increasing self-confidence and self-esteem.

The process used in this book involves a series of exercises asking you to expand your thinking as much as possible followed by an exercise guiding you to focus, limit, and prioritize the most essential information. In the first step, telling your story encouraged you to expand your thoughts and understanding of yourself. In the process, you connected with feelings, accomplishments, and energy that you may have forgotten or never really owned. Now it is time for you to use all the wisdom and information learned in "Your Story" to define and prioritize your skills.

You can think of your skills in three ways: adaptive skills or traits, special knowledge skills that are learned and specific to an industry or body of knowledge, and functional transferable skills that can be applied in work regardless of the industry or field. Following are exercises that will help you identify your skills in each area.

Adaptive Skills

Adaptive skills are the skills we tend to overlook because they seem so obvious. In other words, you have a knack for doing something that comes so easily to you that you don't at first consider it as a valid skill. Or you have a personality trait that is your best attribute at work. These are the things you take for granted but are often among your strongest skills. It is important that you are able to identify and own them. One of the best ways to get a handle on these is to ask someone close to you, or several people, "What do you see as my greatest strengths or assets?" Or, "If you only had one word to describe me, what would it be?" Another means for identifying adaptive skills is to uncover the common denominator or key character traits that appear several times in "Your Story." Is it your sincerity, steadfastness, determination? Knowing these traits in yourself means knowing what makes your spirit shine. These are your special talents and perhaps your unique contribution when applied to the right setting, people, and circumstances.

Another source for identifying your adaptive skills is your Myers-Briggs profile. Read over your profile again and select words expressing characteristics that best represent you. The Myers-Briggs Temperament Inventory was discussed in step 1.

Listing Adaptive Skills

List the traits and personality characteristics that make you special.

_____

_____

_____

_____

_____

_____

_____

Special Knowledge Skills

Special knowledge skills are often learned in school or require specialized training. You acquire technical skills in your field by following a specific training program and then developing mastery and/or flexibility through practice, whether it is in acupuncture, marketing, computer science, or advertising. Some of the precepts of special knowledge skills can be transferred, but basically that knowledge is of greater value in its appropriate field.

Listing Special Knowledge Skills

Rank each skill with 1 = never, 3 = would consider if (list the conditions), 5 = would love to use again in the future.

Skill	Rating	Conditions, if any

Skill	Rating	Conditions, if any

Identifying special knowledge skills will help you assess which ones you want to use in your next job and which ones you want to drop. This assessment can also be an asset in the job search; you may need to leverage from your special knowledge skills to engineer a transition to the next job. This might mean delaying short-term gratification for long-term reward, but it works. For example, a medical technologist who is totally burned out wants to sell houses. By agreeing to sell medical products for a while, the technician will accumulate the sales skills needed to build a bridge of credibility to the world of sales. With sales experience, it will be far easier to convince an employer to hire you as a real estate agent than it would be if you had no sales experience. You will also be in a far better position to negotiate salary or commission base.

Career Management and Self-Employment Skills

The new employment contract requires a new set of career management and employability skills. Whereas the workplace used to be stable, linear, and hierarchical in nature, now it is fluid and always changing. The new workplace requires preparedness for flexible employment opportunities instead of commitment for long-term job security. This puts a greater responsibility on the individual to think ahead, gain new skill sets, and be able to self-market.

Rank Your Career Management and Self-Employment Competencies

Rank the following from 1 to 5, 1 being "not at all" and 5 representing "mastery."

Managing Change = Managing Your Career

___ 1.   Career Assessment—Today's knowledgeable worker realizes that career management is an ongoing part of one's continuous professional development.
   • You frequently assess and evaluate your proficiency with skills and knowledge.
   • You create learning goals to remain current and informed.
   • You are able to identify, create, and communicate with multiple networks from diverse areas for the purpose of advancing career opportunities and maximizing your resources.

___ 2.   Self-Management—The personal is professional, and the more authentic you can be in terms of work style and personal values, the better for you. Bringing your spirit to work in the twenty-first century requires the ability to promote yourself through commitment to your purpose and your values.
   • You are committed to raising your consciousness.
   • You demonstrate initiative and progress through adversity.
   • You work independently with increasing awareness of the larger community.

___ 3.   Interpersonal and Facilitation—The skills listed in this category focus on relationship-building in acquiring and maintaining work. They are also important in communicating with partners, vendors, and customers across the board.
   • You demonstrate insight into motivating human behavior.
   • You develop and practice team-building skills.
   • You manage conflict and practice negotiation and mediation.

___ 4. Project Management Skills—For the unemployed or the employed, project management skills allow you to work with others to get the job done and to partner with others in accomplishing results.
   - You are able to manage and acquire information and resources.
   - You broker services through partnering and collaboration.
   - You anticipate and practice troubleshooting and problem solving.

___ 5. Planning and Decision-Making Skills—When we are clear on our priorities, we make better decisions, but we also need a clear plan or vision and criteria.
   - You possess the ability to visualize, to plan, and to set goals.
   - You establish a daily structure that encourages individual responsibility.
   - You are able to identify criteria for success and then review and readjust.

___ 6. Leadership—As a leader to collaborators, customers, and other consultants in your field or business community, you excel at creating long-lasting relationships and are a recognized leader in your field.
   - You possess the ability to act as a leader and develop the discipline of building community.
   - You are committed to aligning various courses of action that will empower individuals.
   - You are willing to cocreate and share the results.

___ 7. Computer Technology—The ability to learn new databases and technology, and integrate the latest social media, is a key determinant of successful employability.
   - You demonstrate competence with online resourcing, including social media accessibility.
   - You adequately demonstrate database management and retrieval and word processing skills.
   - You effectively use online research tools to access career and industry-related information.

___ 8.   Growth and Development—There is a need for a plan for continuous self-development and lifelong learning. We need to stay passionate about our subject matter and motivated from within to master these skills as well as others essential to outstanding performance. Mastering this skill set will set you up with a plan for lifelong learning.

- You create a plan and identify resources to acquire new skills.
- You have a plan for developing more personal and professional balance.
- You realize your goals of continuous learning to become all you can be and to reach your potential requires a financial investment.

___ 9.   Creativity and Visioning—You'll need this skill set to initiate new activities and to create a "buzz" of originality to your products and services.

- You quickly respond and act on something so compelling that is right in front of you.
- You intuitively know what can and must be done.
- You possess the ability to initiate, develop, and maintain ideas, and synthesize, adapt, and improve.

___ 10. Time Management—Time is one of the most personal tools for transformation when you are engaged in work that you love and when you are self-directed. The continuum of activities that you are responsible for on a daily basis requires the ability to manage your time.

- You develop a list of goals on a weekly basis of things that have to be done and somehow stick to most of it.
- You are comfortable with the balance of time spent working "on" the business and "in" the business (building and delivering products/services).
- You manage to accept there will be days when you don't get enough done but acknowledge what you did accomplish.

Functional Transferable Skills

Functional transferable skills are learned and then further developed in the workplace and in volunteer activities. They are the functions performed to accomplish tasks and complete objectives. These include interpersonal skills—the incredibly important skills of getting along with others—the ability to organize a project and implement a plan, the ability to read and apply printed matter. These are skills that transfer with you from one career setting to another.

Skills Inventory Guidelines

Whichever assessment exercise you chose (Life work Autobiography, Lifeline, Accomplishments Inventory, or Spiritual Autobiography), choose six accomplishments from it for analysis in the Skills Inventory. A broad range of experiences works best. Obviously work accomplishments are important, but outside-of-work accomplishments might indicate different skills you would like to own. There is value in going through the entire inventory for each accomplishment. As a result you will uncover more functional transferable skills and increase the insight and vocabulary gained from this exercise. Your consciousness of self will be increased and enhanced.

Write the six accomplishments in the spaces at the top of the Skills Inventory. Start with the first experience and check the box if you used the skills listed in that experience. You don't have to be an expert in a particular skill. If you used the skill, you own it. Go through the entire report analyzing the first accomplishment. Then go back to the beginning of the Skills Inventory and decide which skills you used in the second accomplishment. Continue the process for the remaining four accomplishments. You can personalize this inventory in any way that would be helpful to you. If you think of more skills to add to a category or if you want to make up your own category and the skills that go with it, feel free to do so. This is your personal information to help you in career choices.

Functional Transferable Skills Inventory

List six accomplishments for analysis using the Skills Inventory.

1. _____

2. _____

3. _____

4. _____

5. _____

6. _____

Verbal Communication	#1	#2	#3	#4	#5	#6
Perform and entertain before groups	___	___	___	___	___	___
Speak well in public appearances	___	___	___	___	___	___
Confront and express opinions without offending	___	___	___	___	___	___
Interview people to obtain information	___	___	___	___	___	___
Handle complaints__in person__on telephone	___	___	___	___	___	___
Present ideas effectively in speeches or lecture	___	___	___	___	___	___
Persuade/influence others to a certain point of view	___	___	___	___	___	___
Sell ideas, products, or services	___	___	___	___	___	___
Debate ideas with others	___	___	___	___	___	___
Participate in group discussions and teams	___	___	___	___	___	___

Nonverbal Communication	#1	#2	#3	#4	#5	#6
Listen carefully and attentively	—	—	—	—	—	—
Convey a positive self-image	—	—	—	—	—	—
Use body language that makes others comfortable	—	—	—	—	—	—
Develop rapport easily with groups of people	—	—	—	—	—	—
Establish culture to support learning	—	—	—	—	—	—
Express feelings through body language	—	—	—	—	—	—
Promote concepts through a variety of media	—	—	—	—	—	—
Believe in self-worth	—	—	—	—	—	—
Respond to nonverbal cues	—	—	—	—	—	—
Model behavior or concepts for others	—	—	—	—	—	—

Written Communication	#1	#2	#3	#4	#5	#6
Write technical language, reports, manuals	—	—	—	—	—	—
Write poetry, fiction, plays	—	—	—	—	—	—
Write grant proposals	—	—	—	—	—	—
Prepare and write logically written reports	—	—	—	—	—	—
Write copy for sales and advertising	—	—	—	—	—	—
Edit and proofread written material	—	—	—	—	—	—
Prepare revisions of written material	—	—	—	—	—	—
Utilize all forms of technology for writing	—	—	—	—	—	—

Written Communication	**#1**	**#2**	**#3**	**#4**	**#5**	**#6**
Write case studies and treatment plans	___	___	___	___	___	___
Expertise in grammar and style	___	___	___	___	___	___

Train / Consult	**#1**	**#2**	**#3**	**#4**	**#5**	**#6**
Teach, advise, coach, empower	___	___	___	___	___	___
Conduct needs assessments	___	___	___	___	___	___
Use a variety of media for presentation	___	___	___	___	___	___
Develop educational curriculum and materials	___	___	___	___	___	___
Create and administer evaluation plans	___	___	___	___	___	___
Facilitate a group	___	___	___	___	___	___
Explain difficult ideas, complex topics	___	___	___	___	___	___
Assess learning styles and respond accordingly	___	___	___	___	___	___
Consult and recommend solutions	___	___	___	___	___	___
Write well-organized and documented reports	___	___	___	___	___	___

Analyze	**#1**	**#2**	**#3**	**#4**	**#5**	**#6**
Study data or behavior for meaning and solutions	___	___	___	___	___	___
Analyze quantitative, physical, and scientific data	___	___	___	___	___	___
Write analysis of study and research	___	___	___	___	___	___
Compare and evaluate information	___	___	___	___	___	___

Analyze

	#1	#2	#3	#4	#5	#6
Systematize information and results	__	__	__	__	__	__
Apply curiosity	__	__	__	__	__	__
Investigate clues	__	__	__	__	__	__
Formulate insightful and relevant questions	__	__	__	__	__	__
Use technology for statistical analysis	__	__	__	__	__	__

Research

	#1	#2	#3	#4	#5	#6
Identify appropriate information sources	__	__	__	__	__	__
Search written, oral, and technological information	__	__	__	__	__	__
Interview primary sources	__	__	__	__	__	__
Hypothesize and test for results	__	__	__	__	__	__
Compile numerical and statistical data	__	__	__	__	__	__
Classify and sort information into categories	__	__	__	__	__	__
Gather information from a number of sources	__	__	__	__	__	__
Patiently search for hard-to-find information	__	__	__	__	__	__
Utilize electronic search methods	__	__	__	__	__	__

Plan and Organize

	#1	#2	#3	#4	#5	#6
Identify and organize tasks or information	__	__	__	__	__	__
Coordinate people, activities, and details	__	__	__	__	__	__

Plan and Organize

	#1	#2	#3	#4	#5	#6
Develop a plan and set objectives	—	—	—	—	—	—
Set up and keep time schedules	—	—	—	—	—	—
Anticipate problems and respond with solutions	—	—	—	—	—	—
Develop realistic goals and action to attain them	—	—	—	—	—	—
Arrange correct sequence of information and actions	—	—	—	—	—	—
Create guidelines for implementing an action	—	—	—	—	—	—
Create efficient systems	—	—	—	—	—	—
Follow through—ensure completion of a task	—	—	—	—	—	—

Counsel and Serve

	#1	#2	#3	#4	#5	#6
Counsel, advise, consult, guide others	—	—	—	—	—	—
Care for and serve people; rehabilitate, heal	—	—	—	—	—	—
Demonstrate empathy, sensitivity, and patience	—	—	—	—	—	—
Help people make their own decisions	—	—	—	—	—	—
Help others improve health and welfare	—	—	—	—	—	—
Listen empathically and with objectivity	—	—	—	—	—	—
Coach, guide, encourage individual to achieve goals	—	—	—	—	—	—
Mediate peace between conflicting parties	—	—	—	—	—	—

Counsel and Serve	#1	#2	#3	#4	#5	#6
Knowledge of self-help theories and programs	—	—	—	—	—	—
Facilitate self-awareness in others	—	—	—	—	—	—

Interpersonal Relations	#1	#2	#3	#4	#5	#6
Convey a sense of humor	—	—	—	—	—	—
Anticipate people's needs and reactions	—	—	—	—	—	—
Express feelings appropriately	—	—	—	—	—	—
Process human interactions, understand others	—	—	—	—	—	—
Encourage, empower, advocate for people	—	—	—	—	—	—
Create positive, hospitable environment	—	—	—	—	—	—
Adjust plans for the unexpected	—	—	—	—	—	—
Facilitate conflict management	—	—	—	—	—	—
Communicate well with diverse groups	—	—	—	—	—	—
Listen carefully to communication	—	—	—	—	—	—

Leadership	#1	#2	#3	#4	#5	#6
Envision the future and lead change	—	—	—	—	—	—
Establish policy	—	—	—	—	—	—
Set goals and determine courses of action	—	—	—	—	—	—
Motivate/inspire others to achieve common goals	—	—	—	—	—	—

Leadership	#1	#2	#3	#4	#5	#6
Create innovative solutions to complex problems	___	___	___	___	___	___
Communicate well with all levels of organization	___	___	___	___	___	___
Develop and mentor talent	___	___	___	___	___	___
Negotiate terms and conditions	___	___	___	___	___	___
Take risks, make hard decisions, be decisive	___	___	___	___	___	___
Encourage the use of technology at all levels	___	___	___	___	___	___

Management	#1	#2	#3	#4	#5	#6
Manage personnel, projects, and time	___	___	___	___	___	___
Foster a sense of ownership in employees	___	___	___	___	___	___
Delegate responsibility and review performance	___	___	___	___	___	___
Increase productivity and efficiency to achieve goals	___	___	___	___	___	___
Develop and facilitate work teams	___	___	___	___	___	___
Provide training for development of staff	___	___	___	___	___	___
Adjust plans/procedures for the unexpected	___	___	___	___	___	___
Facilitate conflict management	___	___	___	___	___	___
Communicate well with diverse groups	___	___	___	___	___	___
Utilize technology to facilitate management	___	___	___	___	___	___

Financial

	#1	#2	#3	#4	#5	#6
Calculate, perform mathematical computations	—	—	—	—	—	—
Work with precision with numerical data	—	—	—	—	—	—
Keep accurate and complete financial records	—	—	—	—	—	—
Perform accounting functions and procedures	—	—	—	—	—	—
Compile data and apply statistical analysis	—	—	—	—	—	—
Create computer-generated charts for presentation	—	—	—	—	—	—
Use computer software for records and analysis	—	—	—	—	—	—
Forecast, estimate expenses and income	—	—	—	—	—	—
Appraise and analyze costs	—	—	—	—	—	—
Create and justify organization's budget to others	—	—	—	—	—	—

Administrative

	#1	#2	#3	#4	#5	#6
Communicate well with key people in organization	—	—	—	—	—	—
Identify and purchase necessary resource materials	—	—	—	—	—	—
Utilize computer software and equipment	—	—	—	—	—	—
Organize, improve, adapt office systems	—	—	—	—	—	—
Track progress of projects and troubleshoot	—	—	—	—	—	—

Administrative	**#1**	**#2**	**#3**	**#4**	**#5**	**#6**
Achieve goals within budget and time schedule	—	—	—	—	—	—
Assign tasks and set standards for support staff	—	—	—	—	—	—
Hire and supervise temporary personnel as needed	—	—	—	—	—	—
Demonstrate flexibility during crisis	—	—	—	—	—	—
Oversee communication—email and telephones	—	—	—	—	—	—

Create and Innovate	**#1**	**#2**	**#3**	**#4**	**#5**	**#6**
Visualize concepts and results	—	—	—	—	—	—
Intuit strategies and solutions	—	—	—	—	—	—
Execute color, shape, and form	—	—	—	—	—	—
Brainstorm and make use of group synergy	—	—	—	—	—	—
Communicate with metaphors	—	—	—	—	—	—
Invent products through experimentation	—	—	—	—	—	—
Express ideas through art form	—	—	—	—	—	—
Remember faces, possess accurate spatial memory	—	—	—	—	—	—
Create images through sketching, sculpture, etc.	—	—	—	—	—	—
Utilize computer software for artistic creations	—	—	—	—	—	—

Construct and Operate	#1	#2	#3	#4	#5	#6
Assemble and install technical equipment	—	—	—	—	—	—
Build a structure, follow proper sequence	—	—	—	—	—	—
Understand blueprints and architectural specs	—	—	—	—	—	—
Repair machines	—	—	—	—	—	—
Analyze and correct plumbing or electrical problems	—	—	—	—	—	—
Use tools or machines	—	—	—	—	—	—
Master athletic skills	—	—	—	—	—	—
Landscape and farm	—	—	—	—	—	—
Drive and operate vehicles	—	—	—	—	—	—
Use scientific or medical equipment	—	—	—	—	—	—

Now that you have finished the Skills Inventory, you will see that some skills, perhaps even whole skills categories, will be either heavily or lightly checked. You will probably think that those skills most heavily checked are the most important for your future. Not necessarily. You may be very good at the skill but not want to do it anymore. There may be a skill lightly checked that reminded you of other experiences when you used that skill and really enjoyed it. Or, when thinking over a lightly checked skill, you may realize that you would prefer to use that skill but haven't had much of an opportunity to do so up to this point in time. Look over your entire Skills Inventory and record the skills to summarize your experience in the Summary of Skills Inventory form. (You can print out this form in an 8.5 by 11 format on our website.)

Summary Documentation

Summary of Skills Inventory

Write in the skills you most enjoy in each of the following categories.

Verbal Communication

_____

_____

_____

_____

Analyzing

_____

_____

_____

_____

Nonverbal Communication

_____

_____

_____

_____

Research

_____

_____

_____

_____

Written Communication

_____

_____

_____

_____

Plan and Organize

_____

_____

_____

_____

Training and Consulting

_____

_____

_____

_____

Counsel and Serve

_____

_____

_____

_____

Interpersonal Relations

_____

_____

_____

_____

_____

Administrative

_____

_____

_____

_____

_____

Leadership

_____

_____

_____

_____

_____

Create and Innovate

_____

_____

_____

_____

_____

Management

_____

_____

_____

_____

_____

Construct and Operate

_____

_____

_____

_____

_____

Financial

_____

_____

_____

_____

_____

Other

_____

_____

_____

_____

_____

Most Enjoyed/Best Performed Skill Sets

It will be obvious to you that your skills fall into clusters. These are your skill sets; give them a name that fits or use the category titles used in the inventory. Then choose eight to ten skill sets that you enjoy most (regardless of the number of checks beside them) and would like to use in your next career move; write them down in rank order in the space provided. Then make a second list of skill sets that you perform best, and write them down in rank order. You will choose from both the "most enjoyed" and "best performed" lists for your portfolio of skill sets.

My Most Enjoyed Skill Sets   **Best Performed Skill Sets**

_____   _____
_____   _____
_____   _____
_____   _____
_____   _____
_____   _____
_____   _____

Training Needs

The next step is to identify any weaknesses or gaps in your skills that you would like to acquire through some extra training. List them now.

Identify Training Needs

_____

_____

_____

_____

_____

_____

_____

_____

_____

_____

_____

_____

Scans Competencies

Compare your skills with five competencies from the SCANS report. Are you well prepared for the future in the following areas? Rank them from 1 to 5 with 1 being "not prepared at all" and 5 representing "well prepared."

___ 1.   Ability to identify, organize, plan, and allocate resources such as time, money, materials, and facilities. Must also be able to assess human resources in terms of skills, evaluation, and feedback.

___ 2.   Excellent interpersonal skills with coworkers and clients: teaching, persuading, selling, negotiating, responsibly challenging procedures.

___ 3.   Ability to identify, assimilate, and integrate information; ability to interpret quantitative and qualitative records; ability to convert information of one form to another.

___ 4.   Ability to understand your work in the context of those around you, understand how parts of the systems are connected, anticipate consequences, identify trends and anomalies in system performance, integrate multiple displays of data, and link symbols.

___ 5.   Demonstrate high levels of competence in selecting and using appropriate technology. Use of technology to monitor tasks; ability to maintain and troubleshoot complex equipment. If ranking yourself on the SCANS Competencies makes you think of some more gaps in your skills, list them in the space with the other training needs.

Now it is time for you to look at the four skills assessments (Adaptive, Special Knowledge, Career Management, Transferable) and choose the skills you want to put into your Skill Set Portfolio. We have included a pie-shaped diagram for you to record your final decisions. Notice the wedge labeled "Training Needs." You may have already discovered some skills you need to add to your portfolio. Put those in the Training Needs wedge now. If you are not aware of any training needed at the present time, wait until you have researched job options and add them then. Once you have accumulated the skills in the Training Needs wedge, you will want to assess what training should be next. Congratulations, you now have a picture of your Skill Set Portfolio.

Skill Set Portfolio

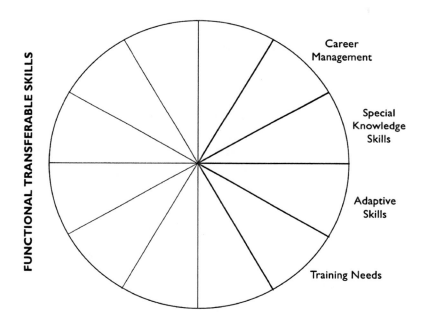

Questions to Consider

1. Are the skill sets in your portfolio broad enough? (You need a well-balanced portfolio of interpersonal and communication skills, project management skills, and problem-solving skills.)

2. Is there a sufficient number of special knowledge skills to anchor your functional transferable skills?

3. Are there several ways you could group your skill sets to make you employable in more than one position? Try filling

out several alternative groupings of skill sets and see what you discover about your potential.

Website Referenced

Academic Innovations (SCANS Report)
www.academicinnovations.com/report.html

STEP #3

Redefining Your Self
Passions, Preferences, and Purpose

It is the longing to know our authentic vocation in the world, to find the work and the way of being that belong to each of us. —*Theodore Rosak*

This step focuses on discovering the answers to the questions posed in the last three quadrants of the mandala. It addresses the concerns: Where do I do my best work? Who are the people that I most want to collaborate with and serve? And finally, why do I do what I do and what are the rewards I hope to achieve?

Assessing skills is the practical part of this process because it provides the vocabulary you will use in introducing and selling yourself in the world of work. Assessing values is the emotional-spiritual part of the process and provides the centering template for decision making and balancing inner psychic energy. Discovering core values and defining one's purpose are keys to finding one's authentic vocation.

My clients love this part of the process the most and find it most revealing. They discover values they never thought about before but that seem so obvious once expressed. Once you know your authentic self, there is no excuse for not expressing it in your daily life. Going through this process of values clarification puts you in charge of your compromises, and that is empowering. When people get in touch with what they need, they are able to assume responsibility for achieving it.

In this step, you will identify what nourishes you in your work, and you will use that criterion to evaluate options in the workplace. When people become aware of what is coming into their life and what is going out, they realize that work has to provide revitalizing energy or else they feel empty. Realizing core values and finding them in the workplace will help make work nourishing psychologically. When these values are realized and combined with skills you love, you will find yourself wanting to go to work in the morning. The feeling of being nourished, fulfilled, and exhilarated intellectually is exciting. Many people who are burned out by the workplace think it is their own fault. They blame themselves for being out of sync with the organization's values, especially if they don't know their own values. Once they are invited to claim their values, they can be more objective in evaluating future options.

Arriving at the core of one's personal value system can serve as an infallible radar system to enlighten and deepen professional choices and activities. Identifying what is most precious and unique about your vision is at the heart of the matter. This step provides eight exercises for assessing values and preferences. Knowledge of personal motivators can guide the selection of employment opportunities as much as application of one's skills. Reflecting on values is the first place to turn when an existing employment opportunity is no longer considered viable.

Going through these exercises will give you the self-confidence to either change or renegotiate your work environment. For the authentic person seeking employment, finding ways of matching your values and the values in the workplace is the most challenging part of the job search. Fortunately, the Internet is a great help; you can do more informational interviewing and viewing of cultures on the Internet than you would ever be able to do physically.

Identifying Core Values and Workplace Preferences

The focus in this section is to identify the characteristics of the work environment and people that are most supportive and receptive to your unique expression. It also serves the purpose of identifying the kind of authority and autonomy you need to do your best work. Clues to the kind of environment you might best function in come from selecting and prioritizing existing criteria; others come from exercises that ask you to envision what your ideal self would desire and then allowing yourself to explore the possibility of receiving that.

What is it that makes work really important to you? What is it above and beyond its most obvious function of earning a living? If something is of value to us we cherish it all the more, and that will affect our attitude toward it. As a result, even the most mundane acts and routines can be imbued with greater meaning. People who are using their talents in work that is congruent with their values have a sense of mission and fulfillment. These people may be fulfilling their soul's task according to Gary Zukav, in his book *Seat of the Soul*. He says: "When the deepest part of you becomes engaged in what you are doing, when your activities and actions become gratifying and purposeful, when what you do serves both yourself and others, and when you do not tire within but seek the sweet satisfaction of your life and your work … then you are doing what you were meant to be doing."

This is no easy task. Unfortunately, there is no one exercise that will neatly tie up a value package for everyone. In fact, there are more exercises in this step than any other, and that is not by accident. Each exercise taps your values at a different level, giving you more and more information about what is important to you. The variety of exercises is designed to work for everyone—young and old, left and right-brained, introverts and extroverts, freelance artists and organizational men and women. We encourage you to do each exercise and determine later its value and worth in the overall definition of you. There is a worksheet for each exercise included at the end of this step and on our website, www.lifeworktransitions.com.

What makes each one of us unique is the sum totality of our individual nuances, beliefs, attitudes, and personal expressions. Your thoughtful and spontaneous response to each one of these exercises will provide you with the information needed to translate your dreams into your life work.

Work Values: Rating Satisfactions from Work

This exercise is essential to the process. I often use it in the first session to get people started thinking about what is most important to them in their choice of career. After completing the inventory, you will want to expand your thinking about some of the items you considered important. If "helping society" ranked high on your list, you can generate new possibilities and personalize the values by brainstorming your responses to the following questions:

- What aspect of society do I wish to see improved?
- Who do I really want to help and how can I be most helpful?

After you have identified the top values (3s and 4s) visualize what that would look like to you. How do you want to have that value expressed in your work life? Or if not in your work life, what other parts of your life should be sure to reflect that value? If other values come to mind now, please feel free to add these to the list of core criteria, to be reviewed at a later date for inclusion in your personal mandala and life work objective.

Motivating Factors

The next worksheet will help you identify other motivators and rewards. If you experience some redundancy as a result of these exercises, it indicates that your values are consistent. In order to get the most out of this next exercise, think of what is most important to you now and prioritize the top five. Sometimes people wonder about the consistency of their values. If you have been in a traumatic work situation, you may identify some value as being important because its presence or absence contributed to the difficulties you just experienced. By completing the various exercises here you will have the opportunity to double-check and verify how lasting these values are. When you actually create your personal mandala (step 5), you will have another opportunity to review these values and determine what really is most important to you.

Factors in the Workplace

In this exercise you will identify from your own work experience the factors in the workplace that provide motivation. Most people enjoy the opportunity to revisit the past one more time to glean important criteria that contributed to success. You may be able to complete this exercise just by reflecting upon your past, or you may find it helpful to reread what you have written to refresh your memory. Individual clients seem to take great pleasure in this exercise because it serves to bring closure on old, outdated patterns that no longer work.

Preferred People Characteristics, Physical Environment, Structure of Authority, Emotional Climate/Corporate Culture

There are four different categories of workplace factors to be identified. Begin by listing the negative characteristics of the following components of your past work environments. Some of you may have trouble with this approach but, trust us, it is healing to let those negatives surface. Listing the negatives first will help you unload a lot of anger and criticism you may hold toward difficult situations and free you to be creative and open in the next step of the process.

The first area for you to identify is the negative characteristics of the **People** with whom you worked, your colleagues and customers. What fun to be given permission to be outrageous and call them what they really are! For example, when you are considering the people characteristics, visualize the nastiest customer or boss you have experienced, and vent your true feelings.

The **Physical Environment** includes listing the positive and negative characteristics of the physical settings and the attributes within that environment. Think about the type of building and office space, the length of commute, and the availability of resources and ease with which you can access them.

The next area for you to consider is the **Structure of Authority** demonstrated in previous work environments where you did your best and worst work. This exercise asks you to identify your own preferred work style and includes such items as autonomy, the ability to self-direct and plan, and how comfortable you are working under pressure. Is your preferred environment team-oriented or is the lone-wolf given status and preference? Think of the least creative and supportive environment and list those factors first.

The last factor to be considered is the **Emotional Climate/Corporate Culture**. What kinds of emotions were triggered in your last job? What kind of communication existed between employees? Was there an atmosphere of trust? Was professional development encouraged? What was the employee morale? What was the predominant management style? How did things get done? What behaviors were rewarded?

After you have gotten all those negatives off your chest, list the positives of each factor in the workplace. The positives are not always exact opposites, and sometimes the order in which you list things is revealing. After you have created both lists, restate the negatives positively. Now you can prioritize the long list of positive values. This list should include the items most essential in that ideally supportive future work environment. Following is an example for defining your preferred corporate culture.

Negatives	*Positives*
• cold, impersonal environment	• friendly atmosphere at outset
• low morale	• mentor as boss
• little informal communication	• plan my own work
• no professional development	• collegial atmosphere

Negatives into Positives
- Cold, impersonal environment *becomes* friendly atmosphere
- Low morale *becomes* all employees feel ownership
- Little informal communication *becomes* regularly scheduled social events
- No professional development *becomes* training is financially supported

Out of your final list of eight positives for Corporate Culture, select the top three; for example, 1. Collegial atmosphere, 2. Training is supported and encouraged, 3. Employee ownership is valued. Add these to your mandala.

My Fantasy Work Day
The next exercise, My Fantasy Work Day, may provide additional reinforcement to some of your previous criteria. It can also offer a totally new picture—an "aha" if you will—that produces an awareness of what you are really looking for. Whether the results are specific in the form of the details generated, or total as in a complete

new visualization, this exercise usually provides valuable insight. Many clients cite this as the picture they carry with them of what their ideal job will be at an unconscious level. Note that there is an important step of prioritizing your indispensable (I) criteria that you'll want to include in your personal mandala.

Ideal Job Specifications

This exercise differs from the previous one in that you may find yourself being more practical. Even though you are asked to identify the ideal characteristics of the job, the ideal here means realizable in the not too distant future. This picture may be more concrete and serve as an initial attempt to summarize the information you have gathered thus far. It does not necessarily indicate the actual job you will be doing, but it offers a template that when realized would make you very happy.

After completing this exercise, use the words you have uncovered to describe the ideal job. You will have an opportunity to create a more thorough life work objective in step 5 that summarizes all the information in your personal mandala. At this stage you are still gathering important information about core values and workplace preferences.

Discovering Personal Purpose

Discovering meaning or finding purpose in what we do is one of the most spiritual exercises in which we can engage. Some people come by this search naturally and seem to know intuitively how to bring clarity and focus to whatever they do. Others are hoping to realize what is meaningful as a result of going through our process. Irene de Castillejo, a Jungian therapist, speaks in her book *Knowing Woman* of an inner clarity as the conscious awareness of being "on one's thread, knowing what one knows, and having an ability quite simply and without ostentation to stand firm on one's inner truth." She goes on to say, "I like to think of every person's being linked to God from the morning of birth to the night of his death by an invisible thread, a thread which is unique for each one of us, a thread which can never be broken." Defining this thread and understanding your personal purpose can provide guidance and influence to a myriad of professional activities. Your unique presence in the marketplace will be defined by your personal vision, your values, and your sense of purpose. Your leadership style will be enhanced with a clearly defined personal purpose statement.

Moving beyond the physical and immediately practical values to the metaphysical, the remaining exercises in this step will help you focus on defining your purpose and how that can manifest in your life work or your personal life. James Hillman, in *The Soul's Code*, refers to the individual's calling as the acorn image or blueprint in us that is an archetype of who we are and why we are here. What is the one thing you *must* try to express or accomplish? Defined in general terms, it can be fulfilled through work or nonwork activities. The metaphor of the acorn or the invisible thread can be a core image for you that manifests itself in different ways. Understanding and acting upon your personal purpose can bring rich meaning and fulfillment.

What Needs Doing in Your World by Others?

This first exercise that has us explore purpose is one of our favorites from John Crystal, and it really works at defining what you see as the world's "deep hunger." The question "What needs doing in your world by others?" is a key to discovering your unique perspective. The idea behind the exercise is to generate a list of as many problems as you can without feeling like you have to have a solution. Great ideas can lead to wonderful places in and of themselves. Let your imagination soar; it and you are limitless. These ideas show in part what you value. We can choose to support these values in our work, our volunteer experience, or in our personal lives.

The exercise has you first list all those things you would have others do to improve our society or the world. This prevents you from ignoring a good idea just because you don't think you would actually know how to proceed. The follow-up is to select one idea that you might be willing to work on and see what you come up with as an approach to this particular problem. How would you tackle it? Are you the planner, manager, or implementer? What needs to happen next? Be as detailed or as profound as you like, or light and sketchy—whatever works for you. This will give you an indication that you may have more knowledge or power than you realize in a particular area. It might provide a clue to some totally new direction.

Ninetieth Birthday Feature Article

The next exercise will encourage you to envision what has not yet shown up in your life and begin to think about including it in your future. In it you'll pretend it is your ninetieth birthday and the local newspaper is doing a feature article on you. In this exercise you are asked to imagine and describe the many personal and professional accomplishments of your lifetime. What have you done over the years? You have already written your life story up until now, so continue the story as only you can. Be sure to include family and volunteer experiences along with work-related successes. What is the tone? Are you fulfilled? Did you work long and hard at something, or meet with overnight success and then move on to something else?

Discovering Your Personal Purpose

Most people find this exercise thought-provoking and stimulating. Your response to the questions gives you the opportunity to review aspects of your past in another fashion and to use your vocabulary to create a powerful purpose statement. By completing this exercise, you will have defined your purpose for yourself in meaningful soul language. This is not something necessarily shared, especially in an interview, but knowing it means you can select where and when to disclose it.

After you have completed the exercise, you will be able to refer to your haiku as a centering exercise when deciding whether to undertake a certain project or client. Each time you use your purpose statement you can reevaluate its meaning and relevance. If you get to the point where you are visiting your purpose on a daily basis to check out the rightliveliness of an endeavor, you will become deeply intimate with it. If it is no longer true or working for you, recreate a new one the next time you visit this work. We are constantly changing and growing and one of the benefits of living on purpose is to be able to take responsibility and be purposeful in our pursuit of rightlivelihood.

Purpose is one of several values you may like to incorporate in work. Not everyone has to have their purpose fulfilled through their work, but their values must be met. One of our clients is a superb flutist who recognized that she was not going to be able to make a living as a professional musician. Her next step was to get an MBA and became a consultant, traveling all over the world. She loved it because of the time it gave her to practice the flute. After marrying, she no longer wanted to be on the road. She was able to rearrange her skills and knowledge in such a way that work would incorporate her changing values. She had an opportunity to be an equity analyst in a nine-to-five job. She chose the firm after researching what kinds of boards were supported by top officers. She chose a firm whose senior executives were on the boards of the Boston Symphony and other arts organizations. With her new time schedule, she was able to perform her work in a setting where the corporate values mirrored her personal values. Likewise, this new nine-to- five job left time for playing in the local symphony orchestra and becoming a mother. She achieved her purpose of pursuing meaningful work that incorporated the balance required to fulfill her new family responsibilities.

Exercises

Worksheets for the following exercises can be found at the website www.lifeworktransitions.com.

BOX 3.1

Work Values

The following list describes a wide variety of satisfactions that people obtain from their jobs. Look at the definitions of these various satisfactions and rate the degree of importance that you would assign to each for yourself, using the following scale.

1 = Not important at all	2 = Not very important
3 = Reasonably important	4 = Very important in my choice of career

---

94

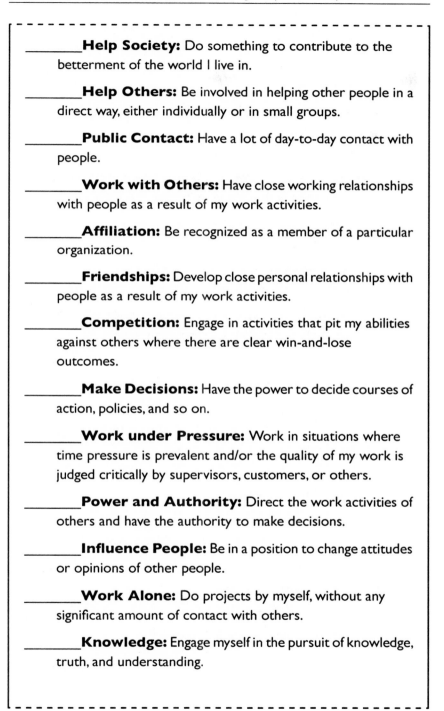

_____**Help Society:** Do something to contribute to the betterment of the world I live in.

_____**Help Others:** Be involved in helping other people in a direct way, either individually or in small groups.

_____**Public Contact:** Have a lot of day-to-day contact with people.

_____**Work with Others:** Have close working relationships with people as a result of my work activities.

_____**Affiliation:** Be recognized as a member of a particular organization.

_____**Friendships:** Develop close personal relationships with people as a result of my work activities.

_____**Competition:** Engage in activities that pit my abilities against others where there are clear win-and-lose outcomes.

_____**Make Decisions:** Have the power to decide courses of action, policies, and so on.

_____**Work under Pressure:** Work in situations where time pressure is prevalent and/or the quality of my work is judged critically by supervisors, customers, or others.

_____**Power and Authority:** Direct the work activities of others and have the authority to make decisions.

_____**Influence People:** Be in a position to change attitudes or opinions of other people.

_____**Work Alone:** Do projects by myself, without any significant amount of contact with others.

_____**Knowledge:** Engage myself in the pursuit of knowledge, truth, and understanding.

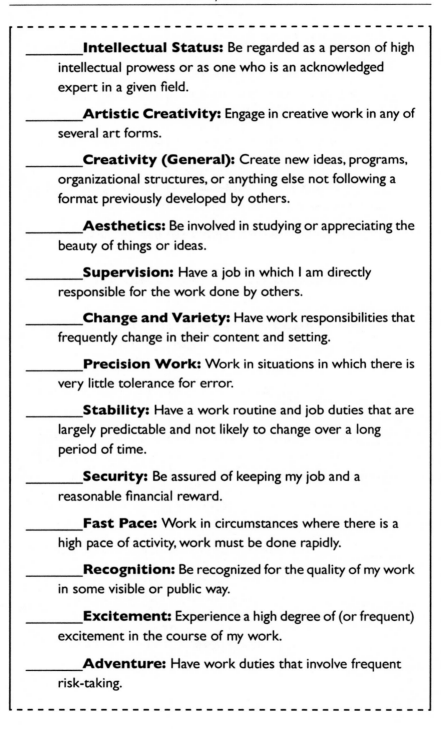

_____**Intellectual Status:** Be regarded as a person of high intellectual prowess or as one who is an acknowledged expert in a given field.

_____**Artistic Creativity:** Engage in creative work in any of several art forms.

_____**Creativity (General):** Create new ideas, programs, organizational structures, or anything else not following a format previously developed by others.

_____**Aesthetics:** Be involved in studying or appreciating the beauty of things or ideas.

_____**Supervision:** Have a job in which I am directly responsible for the work done by others.

_____**Change and Variety:** Have work responsibilities that frequently change in their content and setting.

_____**Precision Work:** Work in situations in which there is very little tolerance for error.

_____**Stability:** Have a work routine and job duties that are largely predictable and not likely to change over a long period of time.

_____**Security:** Be assured of keeping my job and a reasonable financial reward.

_____**Fast Pace:** Work in circumstances where there is a high pace of activity, work must be done rapidly.

_____**Recognition:** Be recognized for the quality of my work in some visible or public way.

_____**Excitement:** Experience a high degree of (or frequent) excitement in the course of my work.

_____**Adventure:** Have work duties that involve frequent risk-taking.

_____**Profit, Gain:** Have a strong likelihood of accumulating large amounts of money or other material gain.

_____**Independence:** Be able to determine the nature of my work without significant direction from others; not have to do what others tell me to do.

_____**Moral Fulfillment:** Feel that my work is contributing significantly to a set of moral standards (to be defined by you) that you feel are very important.

_____**Lifestyle:** Find a place to live (town, geographical area) that is conducive to my lifestyle and affords me the opportunity to do the things I enjoy most.

_____**Community:** Live in a town or city where I can be involved in community affairs.

_____**Physical Challenge:** Have a job that makes physical demands that I would find rewarding.

_____**Time Freedom:** Have work responsibilities that I can work at according to my own time schedule; no specific working hours required.

Now choose six of these work values that are the most important to you. Each will be relevant to the career exploration that you do. If you can think of any other intangible work rewards (desired satisfactions) that are not included in the previous list and that are especially important to you, add them to the six values you have chosen.

1. _____
2. _____
3. _____
4. _____
5. _____
6. _____

BOX 3.2
Motivating Factors

Circle the five items you believe are most important in motivating you to do your best work.

1. Steady, secure employment
2. Respect for me as an individual
3. Good pay
4. Chance for promotion
5. Not having to work too hard
6. Feeling my job is important
7. Attend staff meetings
8. Having a flexible work schedule
9. Lots of free time
10. Having consistency in my job
11. Knowing my supervisor trusts me
12. Working by myself
13. Prestige
14. Growth potential with the company
15. Financial support for lifelong learning program
16. Being able to participate in the decisions that affect me
17. Knowing I will be held responsible for my own performance
18. Freedom to make decisions without approval from supervisor
19. Good physical working conditions
20. Up-to-date technology and resources
21. Chance to turn out quality work
22. Getting along well with others on the job
23. Opportunity to do creative and challenging work
24. Pensions and other fringe benefits
25. Knowing what is going on in the organization
26. Formal and informal companywide communication

27. The organization's interest and concern for social problems (i.e., ecology, pollution, human service areas)
28. Having a written job description of the duties for which I am responsible
29. Being commended by superiors when I do a good job
30. Getting a performance rating, so I know here I stand
31. Having a job with minimal amount of pressure
32. Agreement with organization's objectives
33. Large amount of freedom on the job
34. Opportunity for self-development and improvement
35. Having an efficient and competent superior
36. The organization's willingness to let me spend time working on community activities
37. Being able to problem-solve in my job
38. Having regular staff meetings to discuss policy issues
39. Socializing with other employees during the workday
40. Other_____

BOX 3.3

Factors in the Workplace

1. People Characteristics
2. Physical Environment
3. Structure of Authority
4. Emotional Climate/Corporate Culture

These are the four different categories of workplace factors to be identified. Begin by listing the negative characteristics from your past work environments. First, identify negative characteristics of the people with whom you worked, your colleagues and customers.

Next, identify negative factors in the physical environment such as setting, light, air, style, and location. The next area to consider is the structure of authority demonstrated in work environments. The last factor is the emotional climate/corporate culture. After you have gotten all those negatives off your chest, make a list of positives for each of the four factors in the workplace. After you have created both lists, restate the negatives positively. Now you can prioritize the long list of positive values. Out of your final lists of positives, select the top three for each factor. (See example in the text.)

BOX 3.4
Fantasy Work Day

Close your eyes and try to imagine the ideal work day for yourself. Don't be concerned with realities—just let your imagination go. See if you can picture, in full detail, what you would be doing. Then open your eyes and answer the following questions.

_____You wake up—at what time?

_____You get dressed—describe clothes.

_____What kind of preparations do you have to make?

_____Do you have to work or do you work because you want to?

_____You are ready to leave for work—at what time?

_____How do you get there? How far is it?

_____Do you do anything special on the way to work?

_____You get to work. Where are you? (city, small town, office park, home, etc.)

_____Describe the work setting.

_____What kind of work do you do?

_____How long have you worked here?

_____What are your hours?

_____What do you get paid?

_____What are your benefits?

_____What level is the job? (professional, management, technical, training, apprentice)

_____Do you plan your work or does someone do it for you?

_____How do you work? (alone, in a group, contact with others)

_____What do you work with? (people, data, things, nature, a combination)

_____Describe some of the people who work in your area.

_____To whom do you report?

_____What do you like about your job or occupation?

_____How long do you see yourself remaining at this job?

_____What is the next move (job step) for you?

_____What are your highest aspirations in this field or place of employment?

Go back over each section and put an "I" for those you feel are indispensable, an "O" for those that are desirable but optional, and an "F" for those that are basically frills.

BOX 3.5
Ideal Job Specifications

To your best ability at this point in time, describe in detail the ideal job specifications you would like in your next position. Include the functions you would perform, the physical environment and emotional milieu, the working conditions, your preferred people characteristics, and whatever else is needed for you to do your best and be your most productive self. The final step in this exercise is to create a tentative definition of an ideal job. I want to use these skills _____ in this kind of environment _____, which would help me respond to the following values and concerns _____.

BOX 3.6
What Needs Doing in Your World by Others

Make a list of all the important activities you think others should do. Include in your list political, social, national, and local concerns. Select one and develop a plan of action.

BOX 3.7
Ninetieth Birthday Exercise

Write a feature story describing your many life accomplishments. Imagine yourself at the age of ninety looking back over a long, rich personal and professional life.

BOX 3.8

Discovering Personal Purpose

On a separate sheet of paper, respond to the following questions thoughtfully and truthfully. You may also print out the entire exercise from the website.

1. What activities do you enjoy performing? (List why you enjoy them and what is enjoyable about them)
2. What are you good at? (list skills, talents, and special knowledge)
3. Think of a specific situation in which you felt successful. Describe the time, place, activity. Write what you were doing and how you were feeling.
4. Think of a time you did something meaningful that was satisfying to you. Describe the situation (as in 3 above) and why it had meaning.
5. Think of another specific situation in which you felt successful. Describe the time, place, and activity. Describe what you were doing and how you were feeling.
6. List three qualities you are proud of, and describe why.
7. Describe your vision of an ideal world if you could make it happen.

Review the above information and circle fifteen to twenty key words or ideas. Summarize the key words, and select the ten to twelve that are most important to you and record them here. At this point it is often helpful to share your answer with a close friend. The images you have recorded and the language used describe what is meaningful to you. To create a purpose statement, use the words in the list you just created to develop a series of reiterative statements until you find the one that resonates with you.

My purpose is to

My purpose is to

My purpose is to

My purpose is to

Because purpose is often referred to in soul language, some people like to translate their purpose statement into a metaphor or haiku that summarizes the essence of the statement. To create a haiku you'll want to arrange the wording from your purpose statement to fit the following formula:

First line (five syllables) —/—/—/—/—/
Second line (seven syllables) —/—/—/—/—/—/—/
Third line (five syllables) —/—/—/—/—/

Example:
Leading, Creating
Fulfilling an Abundant
Universe of Trust

(This exercise is adapted from Dave Morrison and Andre de Zanger and presented at the Creative Problem Solving Institute (CPSI), State University at Buffalo, New York, in 1985.)

STEP #4

Goal Setting

Creating a Life Worth Living

In the process of setting goals, we come to know ourselves. Virtually every cultural tradition holds among its central principles, know thyself. Knowing ourselves, the capacity for reflective self-awareness, is perhaps our greatest personal achievement, at least the one that is important to career success. — *Robert Jay Ginn Jr.*

In the three previous steps, you have uncovered old experiences and accomplishments that revived wonderful memories. You have discovered how skillful you are and expressed your skills in words that define you appropriately for the world of work. You have uncovered what really motivates you internally and externally. Now we have to consider how you are going to put all you have learned into action.

But before that, we want you to take a time-out. You have collected a lot of information about yourself and are about to embark on a time-consuming project, researching a new position and marketing yourself in the workplace. When you commit yourself to a shift or change in your career, it is renewing, exhilarating, and a period of significant personal growth. It is also an enormous addition to your life that will take time and a great deal of physical and emotional energy. If you are already in full-time mode, something has to be modified or you will be exhausted, very stressed, and unable to do a good job search. In general, it is a good idea to follow the rule, "If you add something to your life, you should drop something from your life." This is the time to consider life work balance with a serious look at how the "life" part of you is going to fare with the "work" part of you.

We live in a high-speed society that values working full-time, parenting full-time, participating in professional associations, developing a home, caring for our parents, being a good friend, being significant for a significant other, taking an interest in our community, building a fund for retirement, and now acquiring competency to adjust to a constantly changing workplace. There simply is not time to do it all or have it all.

In addition, some of you may be committing to a career shift or change that is not of your choice. It may have been forced on you because of a reorganization of your company, loss of a job, change in marital status, illness, family crisis, geographical move, or empty nest. All of these losses are great stressors in and of themselves and should not be shoved aside. We recommend that you review William Bridges's three stages of transition which are reviewed in chapter one.

Goal setting helps you get in charge of your life, and time management is an integral part of goal setting. Goal setting provides an opportunity to project into the future, maintain a better balance in your life, and increase effective use of time. It also grounds you and helps you evaluate your life as a whole so that life work balance can be a reality. It helps you decide what to set aside as you add career development and a job search into your life. There may not be enough time to have it all or do it all, but goal setting can help you be in charge of it all.

We have had clients attend goal-setting seminars who have returned year after year. Many have said they achieved their goals even though they hadn't looked at them during the year. The single act of thoughtfully writing goals helped them keep their priorities in mind and their time devoted to the action needed to achieve those goals. We can't emphasize too much the act of writing down your goals. Writing down a goal as specifically as possible, and in the form of an "I" statement, makes goals concrete, as will stating it in the present tense: "I own a house in the suburbs." "I am vice president of marketing for a high-tech firm in Silicon Valley." "I am fully trained in the basics of computer technology." Writing down your goals makes them concrete and preserved in your mind.

The following goal exercises will walk you through a goal-setting process. Again, we have included exercises that will help you expand your thoughts and then prioritize them. You will be looking at your life, at this point in time, by general categories with work/career being only one of them in Goal Setting by Life Category. You will be asked to write down your immediate thoughts about work/career, money, lifestyle/possessions, relationships, creative self-expression, fun and recreation, personal growth, and health. The next step is to write a paragraph describing what would be the ideal circumstances in each of the areas. It's okay to create different categories that reflect your personal interests, such as spirituality, community involvement, etc.

The second exercise is a visual representation, a Wheel of Life, with each category from the Goal Setting by Life Category exercise in pie-shaped wedges. The purpose of this exercise is to assess your current level of satisfaction or comfort within each category. You may also want to indicate the amount of time you are spending on each area. When completing these exercises, you will have an enhanced awareness of the critical areas of your life, their importance to you, and the amount of time you spend on them.

Those exercises are followed by one that will help you prioritize what you have learned, focus on the changes you want to make in your life, and state these changes in the form of goal statements. This exercise, Goal Setting: Lifetime Goals, was created by Alan Lakein. To help you get to the core of how you want to spend your life, he asks questions related to time periods. "What are your lifetime goals? How would you like to spend the next three years? If you knew now that you would be struck by lightning six months from today, how would you live until then?" Lakien and every other goals expert stress the importance of writing down your goals. In addition, he feels you can tap into your intuitive side by writing within a limited time period. At the end of the exercise, you are asked to choose your most important goals and prioritize them.

Tips for Writing Your Goals

When you write your goals there are several points to keep in mind.

1. Write your goals down on paper as specifically as possible. A goal committed to paper becomes a concrete expression of your intentions.

2. State goals in the positive, as something you want, not something you want to leave behind; you can even state it as a goal you have already attained. "I am the vice president of marketing for a high-tech company."

3. Make your goals realistic, challenging, but not discouraging. Goal setting is not supposed to give you a guilt trip or make you depressed.

4. Goals should be measurable so that progress can be noted. Make realistic deadlines so that you can anticipate closure.

5. Keep a long-term focus so that you may learn from the setbacks rather than being discouraged.

6. Review your goals regularly; goals are a work in progress and will naturally need modifications.

7. Prioritize your goals, over and over.

8. Celebrate your successes.

The next step in your goal-setting process is to compose action steps that will make your goals a reality and increase balance in your life. Action steps are concrete things that you can do. They prevent you from setting goals that will make you feel helpless. If you can't write action steps for attaining your goal, it isn't a proper goal for you at this time in your life. Writing down action steps for each goal is a necessary grounding activity; you will always know what you are supposed to be working on. Activities from this list can be included in your ongoing weekly list of things to do. You will have things to check off and feel rewarded.

Be sure to reward yourself appropriately for achieving the goal. A well-deserved and much enjoyed reward might include a visit to a favorite bed and breakfast, or a frozen drink on a hot afternoon. You will be more motivated to achieve your goals if there is a meaningful reward at the point the goal is realized.

Presumably one of your most important goals is getting a new job, changing careers, trying to figure out what graduate program would be best for you, or exploring the vocational world to identify options for yourself. This book will help you with all the action steps. For example:

Goal: I am a nurse practitioner for a family practice in rural Arizona by the time I turn fifty.

Action Steps:
1. Study the industry of health care.
2. Learn about being a family nurse practitioner.
3. Talk to a pediatrician in rural family practice.
4. Compare and contrast the various programs and specialties.
5. Enroll in and complete the program.
6. Take care to select internships that match your specific area of interest.
7. Check out the economy and opportunities in similar rural settings.
8. Find specific job opportunities using the net and professional associations.
9. Write resume and cover letters.
10. Interview for the job. Negotiate a salary and benefits package.
11. Take the job and prepare for the next.

Within each action step can be a number of other action steps. Writing down your goals and action steps at each point in the process will very likely ensure that they will happen. In addition, you will be able to measure your progress, stay focused on the long-range goal, and ultimately celebrate your success.

We recommend that you keep a notebook in which you write your goals in the form of a working draft. Goal statements, if they are any good, are always an ongoing process. They will evolve as you gather more information and as major changes occur in any area of your life and in the lives of people close to you. If one of your goals is not serving you, it is okay to give it up.

Repeating the goal-setting process at least once a year is a good idea; many people use their birthday as a reminder. You may want to set goals once, twice, or three times a year, which is terrific. You may want to have an overall plan for your life and, in addition, set specific goals for yourself each week or each day. The process of goal setting is the same at any level. These intermediary goal-setting activities should not interfere or conflict with your overall lifetime goals. Rather, they will enhance the original list.

When you finish the exercises in this step, you will have an overall working plan, focusing on the changes you want to make in your life. This plan will result in easier decision making and consequently better time management. Reward yourself each time you accomplish an action step. You deserve it! Before you know it, you will have attained your goals.

BOX 4.1
Goal Setting by Life Category

1. Very quickly write down what you would do to change or improve circumstances immediately in each area of your life.
2. Then write a detailed paragraph about the ideal circumstances for each area. Dare to dream. Explore in fullness your desires.

Work and Career
Money
Creative Self-Expression
Relationships
Health
Personal Growth
Fun and Recreation
Lifestyle/Possessions
Other

(Adapted from *Creative Visualizations* by Shakti Gawain.)

Figure 4.1 Wheel of Life
(Adapted from The Coaches Training Institute)

The eight sections in the wheel of life represent balance. Visualize the center of the wheel as 0 and the outer edge as 10, and rank your level of satisfaction with each area by drawing a line to create a new outer edge. The new perimeter of the circle represents the current balance within your life. How bumpy would the ride be if this were a real wheel? Draw a second line to indicate how much effort you devote to each area now. Then create an action plan to increase your satisfaction in those areas most important to you right now. It's okay to create new categories within the wheel that represent a more accurate picture of your life choices.

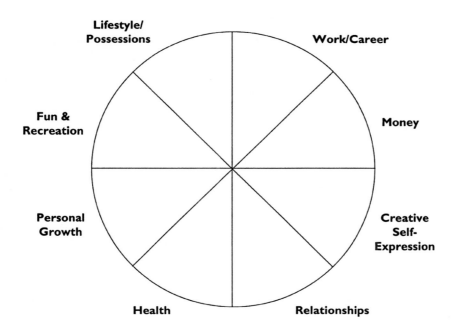

BOX 4.2

Goal Setting: Lifetime Goals

Give yourself two minutes to answer the first question. Your immediate response is valuable. Then take another two minutes to make any revisions necessary to make the statements feel right to you. Go through the same process for questions #2 and #3. Then prioritize your listings in #4.

1. What are your lifetime goals?
2. What are your three- to five-year goals?
3. What do you want to accomplish in the next six months?
4. Go through your goals statements for the first three questions and develop a priority listing. What is most important to you?

(Adapted from *How to Get Control of Your Time and Life* by Alan Lakein.)

STEP #5

Pulling Together Your Profile

A Mandala for Success

There is one elementary truth, the ignorance of which kills countless ideas and splendid plans: that the moment one definitely commits oneself, then Providence moves too. All sorts of things occur to help one that would have never otherwise occurred. I have learned a deep respect for one of Goethe's couplets:

"Whatever you can do or dream, you can, begin it.
Boldness has genius, power and magic in it."

—*W. H. Murray*

The focus of this book, thus far, has been on finding and redefining "right livelihood" as a vehicle for self-realization, fulfillment, and economic independence. The culmination of the process of self-assessment is to create a new definition of yourself, and this step provides you with the opportunity to reflect again, reprioritize your core criteria, and create a visual profile that is truthful and accurate. What does this new definition of you look and feel like? Now is the time to find out.

In pursuit of "finding your true north," we have chosen the multifaceted mandala with four quadrants at the core for you to fill in your criteria. *Mandala* is a Sanskrit word meaning center, or circle. It conveys the notion that any center is tied to its circumference and any circumference is always determined by its center. Together they represent wholeness. (See Figure 5.1 at the end of this step.)

In the upper left quadrant, you will review and record the information about **what** you like to do and do well. It will hold your functional/transferable skills and your multiple skill sets, your special knowledge areas, and your career management competencies. The lower left quadrant will contain all the information you have gathered about the structure, the environment, and the setting **where** you will do your best work. In the lower right quadrant, you will record the information describing the kinds of people, their characteristics and values, that best define **who** you enjoy working with. And finally, in the upper right quadrant, you will record your insights about **why** you do what you do, the rewards and aspirations that will give purpose and create a sense of fulfillment.

Your one-page personal profile defines the conditions that will nurture you in work, make you eager to get to work each morning, and feel exhilarated intellectually and mentally at the end of the day. Most people spend more waking hours in their job than in any activity. If you work in an environment that only takes from you, an environment that requires you to give in ways untrue to your sense of self, you will be exhausted. Many people have very well-paying jobs with lots of security that leave them lifeless, uninspired, and tense at the end of the day. However, if you commit to the criteria in your profile while choosing your work, the opposite will occur. You will perform your responsibilities, *and* you will also be receiving a great deal personally from your job, colleagues, and setting. You will feel enriched rather than empty, have the energy to perform well, and also have a life after work.

You may use the mandala design provided at the end of this step or you may create your own. We have had clients return their profiles on one page of paper in outline form, in a ten-page poem, as a quilt, as web pages, as interactive multimedia games, and as paintings. Whatever works for you is just fine, and we encourage it, but a summary on one page in addition to the work of art is very useful. This one-page profile will be a definition of who you are in terms of your skills, strengths, values, and goals. The mandala will provide the criteria by which you will judge and choose work opportunities and puts you in charge of key compromises inevitable in any job search. The mandala will provide you with the blueprint of what you need to feel fulfilled and continue the journey for this life work transition.

What Do I Like to Do? *(Upper Left Quadrant)*

Turn to step 2 and review your final list of your **Functional/Transferable Skills** sets (refer to Figure 2.1). How do they look? Do they present you accurately? Are they a true, honest, and sincere expression of what you do best? It is permissible to alter or change your skills list now based on insights from this process. For example, review the Fantasy Work Day Exercise in Box 3.4 and look at any indispensable (I) criteria you identified that reflects your interest in what you do, what you work with, and so on. Should this information be incorporated? This kind of flexibility exists now and throughout the remainder of this process. What about the **Special Knowledge** areas? (Refer to Figure 2.1.) List those areas of expertise that you bring to the table. Test yourself by asking, "Is this the kind of knowledge and expertise I want to further develop and hone through my life work?" List these now. You should also list out the **Career Management and Self-Employment Competencies** that will bring added value to the workplace. While you are reviewing this list, be sure to select a Training Goal from the list of skills to be developed from Figure 2.1 and insert at the bottom of your mandala in the appropriate place. Congratulations, you have just created a current and comprehensive profile of your skills, knowledge, and abilities that you can rearrange into multiple portfolios to bring to the workplace.

Where Will I Do My Best Work? *(Lower Left Quadrant)*

Now let us turn our attention to listing the criteria that will define the ideal work setting, and the kind of structure and support you need to do your best work. In the lower left quadrant, you will record the information that will describe your preferences about working conditions and workplace values. Turn to step 3 to review and select the criteria that will describe your preferences in the categories listed. Use these categories as guidelines for completing this quadrant of your mandala and use your imagination to envision the ideal setting. Many times clients ask us to be more specific about what information goes where in this final mandala. But let us say, once again, that it is not easy to tie up a values package. We invite you to return to the simple question of **where** will I do my best work and get grounded while sorting through your information. Be sure to refer to your MBTI results to fill in additional criteria that seem important to you at this point.

- **Emotional Climate:** Describe here your preferred style of leadership in relation to such issues as autonomy, authority, personal and professional ethics, the morale of the place, and so on. Refer to step 3 and the results of your MBTI.

- **Work Environment:** Describe here the factors that contribute to a harmonious, supportive work environment, such as a flexible schedule, the pace of work, etc. Refer to step 3.

- **Structure of Authority:** List here the information that describes how you like to work in relation to others, your criteria that will define the right amount of structure, control, deadlines, and access to resources. Refer to step 3 and the results of your MBTI profile.

- **Physical Environment:** Describe here the length of commute, the location and description of the physical setting, your preferences about travel, hours, and so on.

By defining all the characteristics in these areas you will have the criteria you need to recognize and assess the ideal corporate culture when you see it. Because this area is so difficult to define, it is especially important that you be clear about the information so that you can be flexible and open in how you interpret it and make decisions.

Who Do I Enjoy Working With and/or Serving? *(Lower Right Quadrant)*

In the lower right quadrant, we want you to review and record the criteria that best describe you because your personality factors are an important part of this quadrant. To complete the category **Personal Style**, look at your Adaptive Skills in Figure 2.1 and review the traits from your MBTI profile. List your best traits in this quadrant so that you will be sure they will be recognized and validated by others. Then look at step 3 for the criteria you used to describe colleagues and clients and record them as your **Preferred People Characteristics.** Refer to step 3 to select the **Values** that must be reflected in your ideal setting.

Why Do I Do It? *(Upper Right Quadrant)*

And finally, this rich upper right quadrant must be filled with a myriad of information about what inspires and rewards you. Think of these factors that will provide meaningful **rewards** in terms of **intangibles** — the values and motivators such as recognition, sense of accomplishment, being able to influence others, intellectual status — and the **tangibles**, such as salary, profit and gain, and the chance to turn out quality work.

Refer to step 3 and the results of your MBTI. Do you have certain ethics or beliefs that must be incorporated as a **Mission/Purpose** in your work? Review the exercises in step 3 and record your personal purpose statement from Box 3.8. Do you want to work for an organization that serves a mission that is dear to your heart? Refer to step 3 and record what is important to you. Look at and record the results of What Needs Doing in Your World.

This brings to a conclusion the creation of your personal mandala with the physical, emotional, and spiritual criteria that will help you determine your optimal work opportunity. To reassure yourself of the usefulness of your mandala, compare the criteria with a job or accomplishment you loved and with one that was not a good experience. For the position you loved, you will see that a high percentage of your criteria were fulfilled. For the job you didn't like, you will see that a lower percentage of your criteria were met, and you will be tempted to ask yourself, "Why did I take that job?" If you follow the process in this book and commit to the criteria in your personal profile, you will never ask that question again because you will be aware and in charge.

From now on, you will test each position you consider with/ against the criteria in your personal profile. It will keep you on course with your values and goals. Positions rarely yield 100 percent satisfaction; after all, life is a series of compromises. For example, you may give up location for a position offering growth or you may take a job with tuition reimbursement even though the skills required in your job are not in your most enjoyed skills list. However, most importantly, you will know exactly why you have compromised and will never ask yourself, "Why did I take that job?" The best jobs for you will be the ones that closely match your personal profile.

Additional Information

This one-page summary would not be complete without a review and recording of your goals. We have already asked you to record **Training Needs** that will ensure that you are prepared for your next step. Now identify an **Immediate Goal** from Box 4.2 that will keep you focused on what needs to happen in the immediate future to ensure the fulfillment of your life work objective. As we mentioned in step 4, it is important to identify your immediate priorities in order to focus your attention to proceed. What are your short-range, immediate six-month goals?

Refer to Box 4.2 to identify a **Long-Range Goal** that may provide additional focus and direction for determining your life work objective. Is there some area of your life you need to have in balance before you can begin the next phase of your job search? If so, refer to the Wheel of Life in Figure 4.1 and list an area as a **Personal Priority.** You will want to keep this area in focus as you begin the all-important job search exploration process in chapter three.

And finally, this profile would not be complete without a picture of your **Interest Areas.** List five areas of major interest that you identified in step 3 from the Holland Interest Inventory, as well as the vocational areas that interest you from your MBTI profile.

Creating a Life Work Objective

Now that you have all the criteria of your personal profile on one page, you are going to need to distill this information further and write your Life Work Objective (LWO). This functional and organizational definition will be qualified by people, place, and purpose. It will answer the following heart-centered questions:

- What do you most want to do?

- Where will you be best supported physically, emotionally, and spiritually?

- Who do you want to work for and with?

- Why do you want to perform this work?

Here are some examples of life work objectives.

- I want to use my *advising and counseling* skills to *help people with health-related issues in my own business* where my colleagues are *other independents*, my work space is *at home in a newly renovated guest room*, and my values for *family, autonomy, and helping society* will be honored.

- I want to use my *accounting and interpersonal skills* to *help clients with financial planning* in a *small consulting firm* where my colleagues would include *a lawyer and a financial analyst*, where my work space would *be cheerful and organized*, and where my values of *working with others, profit gain, and recognition* would be fulfilled.

- I want to use my *organizational and planning* skills to *efficiently manage employees and the production of new computer applications* in a *fast-paced high-tech company*, where my colleagues are *smart, laid back, and lots of fun*, my work space *is centrally located so that I can always know what is going on*, and my values of *profit gain, knowledge, and leadership* will be fulfilled.

Using the criteria from your personal profile, please fill in the blanks for two life work objectives. Let your personal profile guide you; consider the data you have accumulated and reviewed as an internal blueprint of what you need to satisfy you. We recommend writing two statements, one that represents your dream but may be a little ambitious at this point, and an alternative that would be "good enough" but not necessarily perfect. We recommend you consider

Plan A as a passion or mission that poses a real stretch in the world of work, while Plan B represents very satisfying work that allows attending to the passion in other ways. The two statements could also represent seemingly opposite directions. Both alternatives can and should be explored.

1. I want to use my _____ skills to _____ in a _____ company/ organization where my colleagues are _____, my work space is _____, and my values of _____ will be fulfilled.

2. I want to use my _____ skills to _____ in a _____ company/ organization where my colleagues are _____ my work space is _____, and my values of _____ will be fulfilled.

Please feel free to amend the suggested sentence in any way that works for you. Some clients like to write paragraphs rather than one sentence. If you are already at the point where you can create a life work objective that is very specific with a job title and the names of a couple of companies you would consider, do so. The point is to begin a draft objective that will give you direction in your exploration of work and your subsequent job search. With additional information you will gather in the next phase, you will be writing and rewriting your objective with more focus and additional specifics. It is an ongoing process until your life work objective is realized.

Your inner reflection has led you to the point where you can trust your intuition to proceed. Relax and affirm the rightness of your choices. Perhaps seek input from interested others. But basically, trust yourself and this process enough to make the decision to move on to the next phase of exploration as we approach the world of work.

Figure 5.1 My Personal Mandala

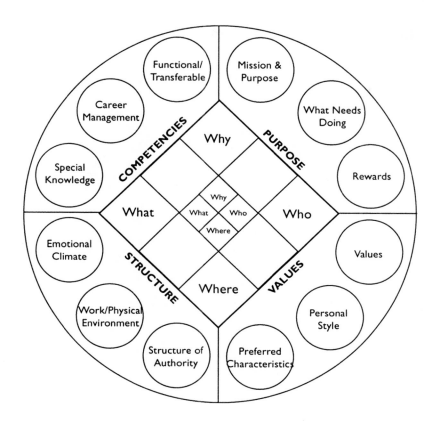

Additional Information

MBTI Type: Goals – Immediate:

MBTI Careers: Goals – Long Range:

Holland Interest Areas: Personal Priority:

3

Putting Your Spirit to Work:
Exploring the World of Work

Congratulations on completing the Life Work Planning process and finding your true north. Having uniquely defined your meaningful work, you are now ready to find the match in the outside world of work. In this final section, we will teach you how to explore the world of work and to identify opportunities for realizing your meaningful work using the four-part model to match your unique Life Work Objective.

Let us refer once again to our four-part model as we make the bridge from the inner exploration (resulting in your Life Work Objective) to the outer exploration of the world of work (graphic Mastering Life Work Transitions Figure 2.1, p. 34). Through a systematic approach, you will gather the information you need to match the four quadrants in your personal profile. This two-part process, (1) conducting career research, and (2) verifying your interests, will result in a thorough exploration of your new world of work. Using the high-tech and high-touch tools of the Internet, social media, networking, and informational interviewing, you'll gain understanding and make connections with the world you want to enter. This two-part process is key to making a successful translation of your personal criteria into a legitimate calling, field of work, or specific job opportunity. The information gathered will help you with branding and creating your own unique presence and profile. As you gather more information, you will be able to refine your resume into a document that speaks to your expertise matched with the demands of a specific industry and position. The thoroughness of your exploration allows you to share your expertise with individuals who can help you and position you positively to be the most informed and valuable resource for "what needs doing."

The first area you will try to match is careers and functions with your description of **what** you like to do, based on your skills and knowledge. Then you will want to explore how the structure and environment of different functions and vocational areas match your preferred working conditions and environment defining **where** you will do your best work. Next you will review and match the characteristics of the people and the values you hope to have met through networking and informational interviewing. **Who** are the people that enliven this field? Would you like spending time with them? Are your unique talents, traits, and curiosity being matched as you meet with others? And finally you will attempt to find a match between what you will find meaningful and rewarding by exploring the vision and mission of the company or the profession you have identified. You will have found the right fit with an opportunity when your reasons for doing **why** you do what you do will be fulfilled. You will know when you are at "true north" when most of the aspects of the new opportunity match your profile.

Exploring the Wide World of Work

In order to actualize your life work objective, created in step 5, you will benefit from our model for conducting research to explore the multitude of options that are out there. According to Sandra Butzel, coauthor of the first edition of Life Work Transitions.com, "For every idea, there is a universe of work." Many clients have said to us, "This statement really sums up who I am, but how is it going to get me a job?" In this step we will help you refine your life work objective in a way that combines the rich internal personal information with the language and customs of the real world of work and a clear definition of your unique niche in it.

We want you to begin the process by having some fun becoming savvy about the wide world of work. Think of any idea that interests you and then ponder the concept, "For every idea, there is a universe of work." For example, one client had strong generalist skills and only one interest that revealed any kind of passion—horses. We took her to the computer and typed the word "equestrian" in one of the search engines. Thousands of possibilities came up: horse riding schools, horse breeding farms, journals and magazines about horses, art collections around horses, horse riding vacations, the whole business and culture of horse racing, and on and on. All of the ideas require people with a variety of skill sets in paid jobs to make them happen. Our client went from a blank state of mind to a list to research that could have been overwhelming if she had not had her personal profile/mandala to help her sort out the best possibilities for her within the equestrian industry. Believe it or not, there is even a job and resume posting site for people who want to work with or around horses, www.equimax.com. If we could come up with so many employment possibilities connected with horses, think of what you could do with marketing, health care, software, or environmental safety.

Researching Career Options Using the Internet

Although it is great fun surfing the Internet and brainstorming with friends to find out what's out there, there are also systematic approaches to conducting market research. You can start your research with any of the steps, but we recommend proceeding through them in order. They take you from the general to the specific aspects of the world of work. Remember to incorporate new information and insights into your life work objective.

1. Your Personal Profile and Objective Statements

Look at your one-page personal profile and your life work objective statements. What are the clues? What directions do you see in terms of what you want to do and where? Your goal is to discover and define where your interests, skills, and values intersect with the world of work.

2. Industries

For example, health, education, manufacturing, finance/banking, agriculture, recreation and leisure, hospitality, government, information technology.

First, cast a wide net to explore industries at www.bls.gov/oco/cg/ that will expose you to the whole world of work. Choose three to five areas or industries that reflect your interests; then verify that these industries have a glowing economic future by exploring trends at www.rileyguide.com/trends.html. There's also an excellent article on trends and research at www.articlechef.com/jobs-careers/article58.htm.

3. Information from Assessment and Internet Tests

Review your MBTI results and the Career Interests Game. Which of the suggested occupations of the Interests Game overlap with those suggested by the Jung Typology test? Which ones seem interesting to you? Check them against the criteria in your personal profile. How do they measure up? Are your ideas becoming clearer? Do you see any patterns emerging? Clues should be building and indicating a direction for you. At this point, you may have chosen a career field that you feel certain is right for you or you may have several possibilities that you are considering.

The next steps will further help you refine your criteria and understand your options within various career fields. For people engaged in specific job search, this research will give you the additional edge of knowledge and expertise that make you stand out in a crowd.

4. Definitions of Career Fields or Vocations

For example, accounting, counseling, public relations, teaching, construction, engineering, consulting, administration, sales, marketing, communication.

In order to increase your exposure to a variety of vocations and test out the ones that interest you, proceed to http://jobsearch.about.com/od/jobsbycareerfieldlist/Jobs_by_Career_Field_List. Or http://jobstar.org/tools/career/career.php. The *Occupational Outlook Handbook* is a standard reference guide and has been the definitive source for both vocational interests and job title information for years. It can be found at www.bls.gov/OCO/.

5. Specific Job Titles

For example, director of public relations, advertising executive, product manager, accountant, hospital administrator, labor lawyer, financial analyst.

The next step is to research the job titles within your vocational interest area so that you can begin to understand the required skills and training for the various positions. Please go to www.indeed.com/ where you can explore jobs, salaries, and trends. You can also start looking at job postings for particular job titles on any of the major job and resume posting sites on the Internet. An even better idea would be to visit field-specific job posting sites at the Riley Guide, www.rileyguide.com/jobs. html#hum for a comprehensive list of sites with job listings. Once again, remember to refine your life work objective so that it responds to the information you are gathering. The information you are gathering will also help you with your informational interviewing as you attempt to get clarity or information from people performing those jobs to see how well it matches these descriptions.

6. Professional Associations

For example, American Historical Association, Institute of Management Consultants, Association for Multimedia Communications, American Society of Training & Development.

Another good way to find out if a particular industry is right for you is to look up related professional associations on the Internet at www.ipl.org/div/special/. Professional association home pages provide all kinds of information such as background of the organization, mission and purpose statements, upcoming meetings, newsletters or journals, and very often job postings. Attending a meeting of a professional association will give you a good idea of the kind of people in this vocation and whether or not you would like to work with and for them.

7. Professional Journals or Magazines

For example, *AdWeek, Journal of Higher Education, Business Week, Modern Hospital, American Scientist, Computer Reseller News.*

We live in an information-based society necessitating a never-ending learning curve, so you'll want to take a look at the professional journals and magazines. They are a great source of information for employees trying to stay on top of what's new in their fields. If you Google "professional journals" and specific topics, such as education or science, you'll find a comprehensive list of specialties to further explore. See if you enjoy the required reading of professions that interest you. One comprehensive listing can be found at www.nova.edu/cwis/vpaa/journals.html.

8. Educational Requirements and Continuing Education

For example, master's degree in education, executive development programs, associate degree in physical therapy assistant, sales training programs, PhD in the sciences.

Besides the required reading for a profession, there may be a required degree or continuing education courses. Research the education required for the job that interests you, which is given at all the vocational interest sites mentioned earlier. Look up educational programs, both undergraduate and graduate, that train for the vocation you are considering. If the training program feels good and fits with the guidance provided by your personal profile, you are definitely on the right track. Go to an open house and meet some of the other people in the same place you are.

9. Specific Companies or Organizations

For example, MSNBC, New York Life, Bank of America, Google.

This last stage of the research process is where most people want to start. They jump into targeting companies and posting resumes on sites without understanding the big picture of the industry. The steps you've taken to get the lay of the land will help you with all of the stages of interviewing to come. The best source for researching your targets is to look up the organization's web page. You can also go to www.careerbuilder.com for national listings by city and category. If you are a serious searcher, you might want to subscribe to Hoover's huge company database at www.hoovers.com. Review company mission, staffing, products, and services, and begin to create a list of features to include as you approach the company.

Congratulations! As a result of conducting this research, you should be quite clear about your number one priorities in being hired or paid for what you love to do. You should also have a much better idea of the opportunities and realities of being hired in that field as well. Be sure to review your resume and update it with additional information. Hopefully you have gleaned a better understanding about the skills and experience you have that are relevant to what is needed in the jobs you want. From here on, you will continue to make choices that will lead you to the job of your choice. The information you gathered on the industry, trends, and educational requirements will continue to inform you in the next phase of your journey and position you as a valuable resource and contributor to others.

Building Your Network—Online and in Person

Researching for information and building your network are essential keys to finding your meaningful work. In this section we will address the high-touch tools of networking (as a verb) and informational interviewing, as well as the importance of using the best of the high-tech resources that social media and the Internet bring to you. For individuals seeking information, contacts, and actual jobs, the use of social media has again given us some new tools to master. The rise of social media in the forms of LinkedIn, Twitter, and Facebook is creating new means for conducting a job search. LinkedIn is the site that has the reputation for being the most professional, but be sure to check out the features of the others as well. There is a great deal of connectivity between them. Bernie Borges, one of the leaders in the use of social media, has this to say about the medium: "Social networking is no longer a fad. The social web is mainstream. Your online reputation, including your professional AND your social credibility, can make or break your job search. Doors can open or close for you depending on how well you network online, make new connections according to the type and quality of content you produce.

In short, how visible you are online and the picture you paint of yourself is not an option. It's a necessity to find your dream job." For more information go to http://www.bernieborges.com/.

For boomers who might be hesitant about using the new medium, all the experts encourage you to take the leap. If social media doesn't lead to immediate job opportunities right now, it will give you better search skills and more contacts down the road. It is the wave of the future, and your willingness to learn it will put you in the place where more hiring is actually taking place. You can learn a lot about each site by understanding how they work, and that requires signing up and taking advantage of the services they offer. It's important to follow through and follow up, as leads can come in quickly and leave just as quickly if you don't respond in a timely manner.

You should have sufficient information now about how to present yourself as a valuable resource in your area of expertise based on the research you have conducted. Use the information gathered previously about your strengths and your new market to translate your experience and create both your resume and your online presence. The information you gathered through the research phase should enable you to incorporate the required skills and knowledge as you translate your experience into your new profile. Remember, never post any information that you would not want a potential employer to view. For more information on the use of social media in job searches go to http://jobsearch.about.com/od/networking/a/socialmedia.htm. You'll want to demonstrate on your profile that you are engaged in your industry and have a unique perspective to share. The information on your profile should be matched by what is on your resume.

Networking and Informational Interviewing

Networking, relation building, friending—these are the buzz-words and the means for finding work and keeping creatively engaged in your areas of interest. Now that you have researched your life work objective and found your true north, you should be centered in the knowledge of what you are seeking, your purpose, and your intended market. Your goal now is to expand your network online and in person to include people who are engaged in that world, building on existing contacts and people you already know. As you build your network using social media, you will have many more people to communicate with regarding your job search and exploration. The traditional tools of gathering information, such as networking and informational interviewing, can be applied to people you've met online as well as in person at local networking events. Make an effort to be connected with people who share your interests in the companies, industries, or fields you have identified conducting your market research

There is a thin line between **networking** and **informational interviewing**. However, we see networking as appropriate for building your contact base and informational interviewing as appropriate for verifying your interests. Networking is more casual than informational interviewing and is most valuable for expanding your personal network to meet others in your field of interest and/or related fields. During networking, you are exploring, building layers of information you will use later when you are hosting informational interviews and when selling yourself during a job interview. While networking, if a contact wants to tell you about a job opening or give you the name of a key decision maker, note the information for your records, thank the person for the information, but hold on to that lead. Too often job seekers talk to important decision makers before becoming thoroughly prepared; this is a big mistake and sabotages your efforts with possibly the most important contact you have made.

Networking is the appropriate type of interview for seeking out individuals who can help you get the lay of the land in your chosen area of interest and job search. Loosely defined, networking is the process of gaining and sharing information, advice, and support from anyone who is a potential colleague, customer, or vendor, and it can take place anywhere people come together. It can take place in your neighborhood health club, church or synagogue, alumni group, professional organization, or online. You can focus your networking by creating a contact list, in which you identify everyone you know related to your interest and anyone you know who might know someone else related to that interest. Then diligently contact each person. Build this network on your LinkedIn account and create a separate spreadsheet to track your contacts and follow-up activity.

One of the benefits of networking is that you will learn more about your potential area of work interest and the people in it. For some of you, it can be fun if you regard it as a continuation of the online research you've already accomplished. You will have more of a sense of control about the job search process because you are taking positive action steps, rather than waiting for something to come your way. You are making something happen for yourself. Most important, it offers you the opportunity to practice presenting and defining yourself and asking appropriate questions. You are building your relationships based on shared interests and hopefully mutual respect.

How you network depends upon your own personality and style. If done online, you'll want to look for introductions from others through your personal network or using one of the groups to meet people. In person, some of you will feel perfectly comfortable walking into a room full of strangers and entering into conversation. The same people will not flinch over calling up strangers for information. Not all of us are blessed with such an outgoing nature, and that is okay. If your style is more reflective, you can go to an association meeting and just listen, maybe pick up some information to read, and observe what is going on. At the next meeting, you might feel more like speaking with people. Likewise, instead of picking up the phone right away, you may prefer to write a note first and follow up with a phone call. Know your style, act upon it, and accept yourself. No guilt trips!

When networking through social media sites, be sure to sign up for the groups that reflect your interests and become active conversing with other experts in that field. Generously share any information you gleaned while conducting your online search that might be helpful to other people. Keep a systematic record of your networking contacts, including their names, where you met them, how to reach them, and any pertinent information you might need at a later date. Get into the habit of asking for business cards. If a networking conversation turns into a rather formal occasion, be sure to write a thank-you note. When you are in your new job, write a note to all your contacts and let them know the outcome of your search. They will really appreciate your note and in the process will become your colleagues.

Informational interviews are somewhat more formal and indicate that you have done your homework and will not waste the time of the person gracious enough to see you. In an informational interview, you should be prepared to present your interests and give some idea of the research you have already done. Explain that you have learned everything that you could about your ideal position but want to verify that interest by talking to someone already doing that job. Make appointments for informational interviews by calling or writing. Follow through and arrange an interview at the other person's convenience for a specified length of time, no more than thirty minutes. Stick to your agenda and be mindful of the time, never exceeding the agreed upon twenty or thirty minutes. Be sure to remind the person you are interviewing that you are not trying to get their job, but to gather valuable information about what skills and experience the position requires. Some useful questions are:

1. What has been your experience in this position; what do you do in a typical day?

2. How is the company or department organized? (An organizational chart really helps.)

3. What was the position you had before this one? Are there other entry points?

4. How long do you anticipate being in this position? What is the career path?

5. Where do you see the field going in the next few years?

6. What training was most helpful?

7. What advice would you give someone starting out?

8. What professional association is most helpful for networking and professional growth?

9. What professional magazine or journal do you feel is a must?

10. Could you refer me to others in the field who might be helpful?

An excellent and in-depth Internet source for informational interviewing is an "Informational Interview Tutorial," at www.quintcareers.com/

The key to the effective use of an informational interview is your own self-confidence and enthusiasm. Think of the other person and create a climate of appreciation, warmth, and trust. Having done your homework, you will be perceived by the other person as genuine and someone who wishes to listen and learn. Most people are willing to help at that level and will share what they know, and hopefully referrals to people they know who are in a position to hire or contract for your services.

It is appropriate, in fact a must, to write a thank-you note expressing your genuine appreciation for the time spent with you. You might highlight what information was most helpful or ask a question that occurred to you since the interview. It is perfectly all right to include a resume with your thank-you note, adding that the person should feel free to share it if an appropriate opportunity exists.

Most of all, remember to be authentic in your presentation and genuinely eager and interested to build relationships based on integrity and honesty. There is so much work to be done in the area you have identified and you'll want to connect with those people who are making a difference in the world. You'll want to add your unique contribution as you find partners, allies, vendors, and customers with whom you will be answering the call to put your spirit to work.

Good luck with your search. I hope these tips on how to explore the world of work will take some of the mystery out of the search in discovering "what's out there." Indeed, there is a world of work, based on what needs doing in your world, and your commitment to finding it ensures your ultimate success. We need what you bring to the world now.

Websites Referenced

Horse Jobs
www.equimax.com

Researching Career Options Using the Internet

Industries

Bureau of Labor Statistics
www.bls.gov/oco/cg/

The Riley Guide
www.rileyguide.com/trends.html

Article Chef
www.articlechef.com/jobs-careers/article58.htm

Career Fields

Job Search
www.jobsearch.about.com/od/jobsbycareerfieldlist/Jobs_by_
Career_Field_List

Job Star
www.jobstar.org/tools/career/career.php

Bureau of Labor Statistics
www.bls.gov/OCO/

Job Titles

Indeed
www.indeed.com

The Riley Guide
www.rileyguide.com/jobs.html#hum

Professional Associations

IPL2 Special Collections
www.ipl.org/div/special

Professional Journals and Magazines

Nova Southeastern University Professional Journals
www.nova.edu/cwis/vpaa/journals.html

Specific Companies and Organizations

Career Builder
www.careerbuilder.com

Hoovers—A D&B Company
www.hoovers.com

Building Your Network Online and In Person

Social Networking for Job Seekers
http://www.bernieborges.com/

About.com Job Searching
www.jobsearch.about.com/od/networking/a/socialmedia.htm

Informational Interviewing

Quint Careers
www.quintcareers.com/informational_interviewing.html

Select Bibliography

Benefiel, Margaret. *Soul at Work: Spiritual Leadership in Organizations.* New York: Crossroad Publishing, 2005.

Bolles, Richard. *What Color is Your Parachute?* Berkeley: Ten Speed Press, 2012.

What Color Is Your Parachute? For Retirement: Planning a Prosperous, Healthy, and Happy Future. Berkeley: Ten Speed Press, 2010.

Bridges, William. *Transitions: Making Sense of Life's Changes.* Cambridge: De Capo Press, 2004.

Brook, Nancy. *Thriving at Work: A Guidebook for Survivors of Childhood Abuse.* Self-Published. Contact *www.authenticwork.com* for price and shipping cost.

Boyett, Joseph and Henry Conn. *Beyond Workplace 2000.* New York: Dutton, 1996.

Buechner, Frederick. *Wishful Thinking: A Seekers' ABC.* San Francisco: Harper Collins, 1993.

Crystal, John and Richard N. Bolles. *Where Do I Go From Here with My Life?* Berkeley: Ten Speed Press, 1980.

Dychtwald, Ken. *Bodymind.* New York: JP Tarcher, 1986.

Freedman, Marc. *Encore: Finding Work that Matters in the Second Half of Life*. Cambridge: Perseus Group, 2007.

Fox, Matthew. *The Reinvention of Work*. San Francisco: Harper Collins, 1995.

Hakim, Cliff. *Rethinking Work: Are you Ready to Take Charge?* Boston: Nicholas Brealey Publishing, 2007.

Handy, Charles. *The Age of Unreason*. Boston: Harvard Business School Press, 1990.

Hillman, James. *The Soul's Code: In Search of Character and Calling*. New York: Random House, 1996.

Hyatt, Carol, and Linda Gottlieb. *When Smart People Fail, Rebuilding Yourself for Success*. New York: Penguin, 2009.

Keirsey, David, and Marilyn Bates. *Please Understand Me II: Temperament, Character and Intelligence*. Del Mar: Prometheus Nemesis, 1984.

Levy, Frank. *The New Division of Labor: How Computers Are Creating the Next Job Market*. New York: Russell Sage Foundation, 2004.

Maslow, Abraham. *Toward a New Psychology of Being*. New York: John Wiley, 1999.

McMeekin, Gail. *The Twelve Secrets of Highly Creative Women: A Portable Mentor*. San Francisco: Conari, 2000.

The Twelve Secrets of Highly Successful Women: A Portable Mentor. San Francisco: Conari, 2011.

Myss, Caroline. *Why people Don't Heal and How They Can*. New York: Random House, 1997.

Palmer, Parker. *Let Your Life Speak: Listening for the Voice of Vocation*. Hoboken: Jossey-Bass, 2000.

Pink, Daniel. *A Whole New World: Why Right Brainers Will Rule the World*. Berkeley: The Berkeley Publishing Group, 2006.

Drive: The Surprising Truth About What Motivates Us. London, England: the Penguin Group, 2009.

Rifkin, Jeremy. *The Third Industrial Revolution: How Lateral Power is Transforming the Energy, the Economy and the World*. New York: St. Martin, 2011.

The Empathic Civilization: The Race to Global Consciousness in a World in Crisis. New York: JP Tarcher, 2009.

The End of Work: The Decline of the Global Labor Force. New York: JP Tarcher, 2004.

Spangler, David. *The Call*. New York: Riverhead Books, 1998.

Ray, Paul, and Sherry Ruth Anderson. *Cultural Creatives: How 50 Million People Are Changing the World*. New York: Random House, 2001.

Tieger, Paul, and Barbara Baron-Tieger. *Do What You Are: Discover the Perfect Career for You Through the Secrets of Personality Type*. Boston: Little Brown & Co., 2007.

Wakefield, Dan. *The Story of Your Life: Writing a Spiritual Autobiography*. Boston: Beacon Press, 1990.

Zukav, Gary. *Seat of the Soul*. New York: Simon & Schuster, Fireside Edition, 1990.

About the Author

Deborah Knox has over thirty years experience offering career and life work planning services to individuals committed to successfully navigating their careers well into the twenty-first century. For individuals seeking to live deeply and with balance, she offers a repository of tools, resources, and models for successfully engaging in the world of work.

As Deborah Knox & Associates, located in New England, she offered programs to corporations and organizations to assist their employees in creating significant career paths. Individuals benefit from her coaching style and knowledge base to discover their true life work.

Deborah relocated to Tucson AZ in 2001 and now offers her programs and services through Life Work Transitions, www.lifeworktransitions.com. She is the author of *Put Your Spirit to Work: Making a Living Being Yourself,* Wheatmark, 2012.

CPSIA information can be obtained at www.ICGtesting.com
Printed in the USA
BVOW04s1411190913

331495BV00001B/248/P